MW01620194

MOTHER OF
ALL GATEWAY DRUGS

PARABLES
FOR OUR TIME

MOTHER OF ALL GATEWAY DRUGS

PARABLES FOR OUR TIME

John Newmeyer, Ph.D.

2007

First edition published by Haight Ashbury Publications,
856 Stanyan Street, San Francisco, California 94117

Library of Congress Catalog Number 2007923156

Newmeyer, John. Mother of All Gateway Drugs.

ISBN-10: 0-9641233-2-0
ISBN-13: 978-0-9641233-2-8

CONTENTS

ACKNOWLEDGMENTS

I am thankful above all to those who inspired most of this work: my colleagues in the Community Epidemiology Work Group, especially Blanche Frank of New York, John French of New Jersey, and Wayne Weibel of Chicago.

To the extent that my words express humanity and compassion, thanks should go to Dr. David E. Smith, founder of the Haight-Ashbury Free Clinic and generous contributor of the Foreword herein. Likewise, whatever economic good sense is found in these pages should ultimately be credited to the writers of *The Economist* magazine.

I owe sincere thanks to Richard Seymour and Terry Chambers for their competent work in editing this work. I would also like to thank Jon Carroll for kindly permitting me to reprint his superb essay.

Lastly, this book owes thanks to Saddam Hussein, whose "Mother" metaphor is so much more appropriate to the sweet milk of human desire than to warfare.

DEDICATION

To all prisoners and other victims of the Drug Wars, I bring this message of hope that the present long-enduring era of *cruelty* will finally come to an end. And to the poor tax-payer who has seen so much of his good money wasted in futility, I bring this missive of hope that the era of *waste* will finally come to an end. I apologize that it has taken me so long to get these hopeful words into print.

FOREWORD

I have had the privilege of working with John Newmeyer for over 30 years, since he began his research as epidemiologist for the Haight-Ashbury Free Clinics in 1971. Since that time John has made many contributions to the addiction field and has taught us clinicians "to look at the forest as well as the trees" in studying the drug problem. In the course of his studies he has become a keen observer and harsh critic of our nation's drug policies. His fascinating work, *Mother of All Gateway Drugs: Parables for Our Time* shares his accumulated wisdom on why our war on drugs has been such a social-policy and economic disaster.

As John puts it, the war on drugs has visited an astounding amount of cruelty upon people merely because they are entangled in addictive disease. It has become clear that there can never be a victory in this war. Essentially no progress has been made in the whole era of John's work– but he remains optimistic that one great morning people like himself will give one last *push* and the whole preposterous edifice of the Drug War will come tumbling down.

David E. Smith, M.D.
Founder, Haight-Ashbury Free Clinics

INTRODUCTION

This book is the fruit of more than 30 years' work as the epidemiologist at the Haight-Ashbury Free Clinics in San Francisco. It's been the major focus of my career since earning my Ph.D. at Harvard University in 1970.

Much of my work has consisted of examining "drug" use patterns and trends, both in this City and in the nation as a whole. I've observed three overarching themes in America's "war" on drugs. First, I've seen an astounding amount of *cruelty* visited upon people merely because they are entangled in addictive disease. Liberals like me cry out for reform and compassion. But we're ahead of our times; the political realities, for now, are against us.

Second, I've also seen 30 years of prodigious *waste* of money: billions wasted on failed drug-control policies, and more billions not gained because we tax and regulate only some of the drugs we should. Conservatives like me demand an end to social policies which don't work, and we insist that taxes on consumption (especially of "sins") are the best, and perhaps the only, taxes a society should levy. But we're ahead of our times; the political realities, for now, are against us.

Finally, it's become clear that there can never be a "victory" in the "war". Essentially nothing has changed in the American drug-use scene that I have so assiduously studied. Initially I felt frustration at this state of affairs; this matured into a profound cynicism, which evolved in turn into an exasperated derision aimed at stupid people in high places. Finally, I broke through into the sunny uplands of *humor*— that happy form of human civilization which, among other things, helped people cope with the grim years of life in the Soviet Empire. It's exhilirating to recall how suddenly that empire collapsed– and to imagine that, one great morning, people like me will give one last laughing *push* and the whole preposterous edifice of the Drug War will come tumbling down.

John Newmeyer, Ph.D.
San Francisco
March 2007

"Laugh out loud– we're happy because we laugh,
not, we laugh because we're happy."

MOTHER OF
ALL GATEWAY DRUGS

PARABLES
FOR OUR TIME

John Newmeyer, Ph.D.

2007

The Mother of All Gateway Drugs

"Imagine a moment when the sensation of honey or sugar on the tongue was an astonishment, a kind of intoxication. The closest I've ever come to recovering such a sense of sweetness was secondhand, though it left a powerful impression on me even so. I'm thinking of my son's first birthday. I have only the testimony of Isaac's face to go by (that, and his fierceness to repeat the experience), but it was plain that his first encounter with sugar had intoxicated him– was in fact an ecstasy, in the literal sense of that word. That is, he was beside himself with the pleasure of it, no longer here with me in space and time in quite the same way he had been just a moment before. Between bites Isaac gazed up at me in amazement (he was in my lap, and I was delivering the ambrosial forkfuls to his gaping mouth) as if to exclaim, 'Your world contains *this*? From his day forward I shall dedicate my life to it.' (Which he basically has done.) And I remember thinking, this is no minor desire, and then wondered: Could it be that sweetness is the prototype of *all* desire?"

Michael Pollan, *The Botany of Desire*
(New York: Random House, 2001)

Consuming Passions

After long years of studying substance use and abuse, I've realized that only eight "substances" really matter. There are of course marijuana, heroin, cocaine, and "speed", the four major illicit *drugs*. Looming over these are alcohol, tobacco, caffeine, and sugar, the four great legal drugs (a.k.a. *foods, beverages, substances.*)

The few who use illicit drugs seem to pursue the same psychoactive effects as the many who make do with the legal drugs, roughly thus:

Psychoactive Effect Sought	Illegal Drugs	Legal Drugs
Stimulation, a "pick me up"	Cocaine, "Speed"	Caffeine, Tobacco
Comfort, relief from pain, "attitude adjustment"	Heroin	Alcohol
Sheer pleasure, a gladdening of spirit	Marijuana	Sugar

Recently I conducted a fascinating exercise: I put a month's "supply" of each substance on a table to see what they'd look like together. I found data in an almanac on the nation's consumption of the legal substances, and I also located recent D.E.A. estimates on consumption of the four illegal drugs. Then I calculated the average American monthly consumption of the eight substances, by dividing overall consumption by population. For sugar and caffeine, I divided by the total population of 297 million, and for the other substances I divided by the total adult population of 221 million (we expect children to consume sugar and caffeinated soft drinks, but not the other substances.) Here are the results, expressed in milligrams per month per American:

SUGAR (pure)	6,100,000 mg.
ALCOHOL (100 proof)	1,500,000 mg.
CAFFEINE (coffee beans)	380,000 mg.
TOBACCO (cigarettes)	210,000 mg.
MARIJUANA (leaves)	300 mg.
COCAINE (pure)	125 mg.
SPEED (pure)	15 mg.
HEROIN (pure)	5 mg.

This "standard American monthly consumption", once assembled on the table, looked like this: the sugar was in 13 one-pound cartons, the alcohol was in two quarts of 80-proof vodka, the coffee was five-sixths of a pound of beans, and the tobacco was 149 ordinary cigarettes. The illicit drugs consisted of marijuana leaves equal to about one-third of a cigaretteful, the cocaine was 1/32nd of a teaspoon of powder, the speed was about 1/8th of the cocaine amount, and the heroin about 1/3rd of *that* amount.

The table groaned under the weight of the sugar. The vodka, cigarettes, and coffee were also weighty, a pound or two each. But the marijuana leaves, about the volume of a cashew-nut, were almost lost in this pile of consumables. And the cocaine, speed, and heroin were of derisory insignificance, little scatterings of grains rather like what you'd see on the table if you knocked over a salt shaker.

This exercise was a vivid reaffirmation that America's drug scene is totally dominated by the four legal drugs. We notice the four illegal drugs mostly because the relatively tiny minorities who use them are vigorously and conspicuously persecuted.

How Much Do We Pay?

When I purchased the four legal drugs, I was surprised to notice that I paid the about same amount for each drug's "monthly per capita share": $10, excluding taxes. Of course there were no taxes on the sugar and coffee, but Federal and State taxes nearly doubled the price of the vodka and more than tripled the price of the cigarettes. Thus, after hundreds of years of competition among growers, refiners, wholesalers, and retailers, the before-tax price of a month's worth of each of the four main drugs has come down to about an hour's wage for an unskilled worker. I reflected on that as I gazed at my tableful of legal drugs: how marvelous that so many pick-me-ups, so much warmth and comfort, such ample gladness of spirit, is to be had so cheaply in our times!

This thought soon gave way to melancholy reflection upon the four illegal drugs. The street costs of the amounts shown in the table are also not far from $10 per person per month, but that's a population-wide average: in reality, maybe 1% or 2% of adults are regular users and each spends about 50 or 100 times as much. Presumably they get the same basic psychoactive effects as the rest of us do from the legal equivalents, but more intensely so (after all, they're smoking crack rather than drinking coca tea, while we're sipping coffee rather than snorting caffeine powder.) They do so in the face of great tribulations, and usually manage to keep at it only so long as the stamina of youth endures. Then they rejoin the rest of us in a docile middle age of Starbucks and doughnuts, booze and Marlboros.

In the Aggregate

The above table can also serve as a handy measure of overall American consumption, simply by replacing "milligrams" with "tons" and changing "monthly" to "every four months" (for sugar and coffee) or "every five months" (for the other six substances). For example, the aggregate American consumption of sugar is 6,100,000 tons every four months; of cocaine, 125 tons every five months. It immediately becomes obvious that commerce in the legal drugs is characterized by huge amounts of sheer labor: millions of people to pick the winegrapes and coffeebeans, staff the factories, drive the trucks, shlep the cases of booze around, restock the supermarket shelves, etc., etc. The amount of labor needed for the marijuana, cocaine, speed, and heroin industries is trivial by comparison. Yet every one of these eight drugs is a multibillion dollar industry in America in 2007. It is obvious, therefore, that the profit margins on the illegal drugs are far greater, if only because the billions in income are distributed among far fewer workers. But there were also big profit margins for coffee, rum, sugar, and tobacco in the 17th and 18th centuries: planters and shippers became fabulously rich because they served insatiable demands of consumers who craved the new pleasures and eagerly paid good money for them.

Thinking About Policy

This book is divided into ten sections, each introduced by a Parable. The first four sections touch upon five of the drugs cited in the table on page 3: sugar, alcohol, heroin, cocaine, and caffeine. The fifth section sets the framework for the policy analyses in the second half of the book. It makes the critical argument that drug use policy has been, and will continue to be for some time, *paralyzed*. The final five Sections address different aspects of America's drug use policies and consequences: "forced" migration, the time bomb of hepatitis C, the role of private enterprise and free markets, strategies for sabotaging stupid policies, and the crucial difference made by drug potency.

Each section is introduced with a parable. This ancient literary form is a handy way to illuminate the section's moral and/or commonsensical truth. There are really only three truths I am getting at in this book; simply put, they are the quintessence of my 35 years of experience in studying substance use as an epidemiologist:

- Virtually all of us use substances to achieve desired psychoactive effects. This is right and good and authentically *human*– our ancestors have done it for thousands, perhaps millions, of years. As noted in the table on page 3, we Americans have eight major choices in seeking the three major psychoactive effects. These choices may differ in potency and legality, but in essence we're all in the same game, we are all "junkies" for one thing or another. (Parables I, IV, and X)

- Given that we're all in the same game, it behooves us to treat one another with *kindness* and *decency*. That is, obey the Golden Rule– the one and only precept common to all the world's religions. (Parables II, III, IV, VI, VIII, and X)

- As we salve our liberal spirit through kindness and decency, let's salve our conservative spirit through *saving the taxpayers' hard-earned money*– that is, choose policies which are most cost-effective in the long run. (Parables I, II, III, IV, VII, VIII, and IX)

Again and again in this book I will urge the reader to take the long view. To study history is marvelously enlightening. Our history embraces so very much: the co-extension of the Roman world and viticulture– the way we spent much of the Middle Ages mildly drunk on beer or wine while eschewing the contaminated drinking water of our villages and towns– the exhilirating smoke of tobacco, first in Elizabethan clay pipes and much later in abundant cheap cigarettes– the way coffee and tea stimulated commerce and Enlightenment in the 17th and 18th centuries– the arrival of cheap sugar, to gladden the spirit at ever-more-frequent breaks during the workday– the amazing, if dismaying, impact of distilled alcohol when brandy and rum and gin appeared on the scene– the welcome solace in our times-of-pain given by opium, then laudanum, then morphine, then heroin, then the opiate derivatives– the stunning spread of good cheer as marijuana made itself a normal part of growing up in America... all of this lovely history unfolding in the light of a corollary to the first of the abovemention truths: "whether a substance is a delightful consumable, or a nasty and evil drug, depends entirely on whose cartel got going first."

I.

The Parable of the Sugar High

Parable I

Bureau of Alcohol, Tobacco and Sugar

News and Information Services **Washington, DC**

WASHINGTON, DC, TUESDAY, JULY 16, 2013– Earlier today, President Luther Sanchez signed HR 2012, providing for a 75% increase in excise taxes on added-sugar foodstuffs. Such foodstuffs– including most 'soft' drinks and cereals– will be liable for Federal taxes averaging 47 cents per ounce of added sugar. Coca-Cola, Inc. and Pepsi-Cola, Inc. announced immediate increases in prices for their principal products, expected to push the retail cost of a 12-ounce can to above $3.

"This adjustment in excise tax rates is long overdue," declared Richard Dutton, BATS Director. "Last year's raise of alcohol taxes to $120 per gallon, and of tobacco to $9 per pack, promptly had the desired effect of reducing youth consumption of these substances. It's sugar's turn now. These three excise increases will enhance government revenue by about $250 billion per year, which will help cut the huge debt burden the nation inherited from the Bush years."

"This measure will go far toward reducing obesity and diabetes in our country," declared President Sanchez. "As the father of two daughters who between them weigh a quarter of a ton, I deplore the grip that the sugar oligarchs have upon our youth. I urge all the States to follow the lead of California, and raise to 16 the legal age for purchase of sugar-added drinks. If we work together, we can at last turn the corner in America's battle on the bulge."

This Parable imagines a future world in which the Bureau of Alcohol, Tobacco and Firearms has morphed into the "Bureau of Alcohol, Tobacco and *Sugar*". As will be argued shortly, the new grouping makes more sense because it envisions one federal department to oversee the three major substances which kill *lots of people slowly*. Firearms can become the concern of the States and their Departments of Motor Vehicles and Firearms, which would regulate the devices which kill *a few people quickly*. Of course, "few" is a relative term, referring to mere tens of thousands of annual deaths as opposed to hundreds of thousands.

Hundreds of thousands of deaths per year translate to millions of deaths ("Megadeaths") per decade. Very roughly, we can credit tobacco with four American Megadeaths per decade, and sugar and alcohol with a bit more than one Megadeath each. Sugar has attained this exalted power because of its role in the vastly increased prevalence of obesity in the past 30 years. Obesity in turn increases the risk of many diseases and health conditions, such as diabetes, heart disease, stroke, osteoarthritis, asthma, gallstones, infertility, colon cancer, and breast cancer. To be sure, fatty foods and lack of exercise are also factors in obesity and diabetes– but our per capita consumption of fats, and our exercise routines, have not changed much in a generation, whereas our intake of sugar has gone up by about a third, from 114 pounds per person per year in 1967 to 152 pounds in 2005[1]. And just in the past decade, we've

---

[1] The Surgeon General in December 2001 issued a "Call to Action" declaring that American's excess weight was killing about 300,000 of us per year. My educated guess is that sugar gets one-third of the blame for that excess weight, hence 100,000 deaths/year or 1 million/decade.

increased our daily per capita consumption of food energy by 200 calories!

The broad masses of the American population are steadily, remorselessly getting fatter: in the past 25 years, the prevalence of overweight Americans has increased by nearly 1% per year. One is misled by the "fitness revolution"– all those diligent Americans jogging, going to gyms, devouring healthy drinks and foods, and looking enviably fit. Look more closely, and one notices that among these fine people is an overrepresentation of the well-educated, the well-off, and (among males) the gay. The last to fatten will be rich White women and rich gay men.

Of all the bad health consequences of obesity, diabetes is the worst. This disease is far commoner among minorities, and above all among Black women and Latinas:

Estimated lifetime risk of developing diabetes, for children born in 2000

White boys	27%
White girls	31%
Black boys	40%
Black girls	49%
Latino boys	45%
Latina girls	53%

(Source: Centers for Disease Control and Prevention, 2003)

It's only fair to blame starches as well as sugar for the diabetes epidemic. When either of these forms of carbohydrates are eaten, they're converted to glucose and enter the circulatory system as blood sugar. As high levels of blood sugar aren't good for the body, the pancreas promptly responds by secreting insulin to counter the surge. Insulin signals the skeletal muscles to take up more glucose from the blood, thus inhibiting the production of new glucose by the liver. Overweight people, however, have muscles and livers that are less sensitive to insulin, so their livers may continue to produce insulin even when their bodies don't need it. The result of this "insulin resistance" can be chronically high blood-sugar levels and, eventually, diabetes.

Maps of obesity prevalence showed back in 1985 that the "home office" of American obesity was in the South Central states of Louisiana, Arkansas, and Mississippi. Twenty years later, these "Fat States" have an even higher incidence of obesity– but California, once the exemplar of "fit America", now has the same prevalence as the Fat States had in 1985. Moreover, Californians are getting fatter faster than are the Fat States– i.e., we are closing the gap.

Thus, America in the first half of the 21st Century is likely to be a nation overwhelmed by infirmity and death related to obesity and diabetes. It is quite possible that our life expectancy, which increased gradually throughout the 20th Century, will reach a peak and begin a slow decline. And naturally there will be staggering healthcare costs consequent upon obesity-related infirmities. Sugar's contribution to all this is hard to gauge, but it is certainly substantial: I estimate that if our sugar intake magically returned to the 1967 rate, the prevalence of obesity and diabetes would drop by one-fourth to one-third.

So, sugar kills, albeit ever so slowly. It is also, arguably, an *addictive psycoactive drug*, which is why I term it the "Mother of All Gateway Drugs". Sugar is *psychoactive* because it alters our perception of the world in an unmistakable way (see page 2). And it meets all the criteria of *addiction*: people think much about how good the next "dose" will be, and continue to use in the face of adverse consequences and in spite of repeated attempts to quit or cut back.

The nasty aspects of Americans' love affair with sugar has been well elucidated elsewhere, for example in William Dufty's excellent *Sugar Blues* (Warner Books, 1986) or in Eric Schlosser's *Fast Food Nation* (Houghton Mifflin, 2001). I will devote the remainder of this chapter to examining our strange *complacency* in the face of the new Sugar Megadeath Era. I've been complicit in that complacency, as a member of one of the country's major institutions (the Community Epidemiology Work Group) charged with the task of gauging the extent of drug use in metropolitan areas of the U.S. The CEWG has convened every six months for 30 years to share the latest research findings on the incidence and prevalence of usage of heroin, cocaine, methamphetamine, marijuana, and a host of drugs of lesser importance such as LSD, MDMA, PCP, and codeine. Over the years a lot of very smart and creative people have worked with the CEWG, and we've developed many clever ways to be an early warning system for evolving trends in substance use– thus to help communities to be *armed and ready* for developing drug problems, for example the spread of methamphetamine abuse from the West Coast eastward.

The CEWG specialized in the subtle arts of discerning trends in illicit, and hence hidden, drug usage. We also kept an eye on trends in tobacco and alcohol use, along with two other institutions– the National Household Survey and the Monitoring the Future Study– that have done excellent work in this area for more than 20 years. But there has been nary a mention in all these years of *sugar* from any of the three institutions. That substance has not been watched, and it has not been fought, with any of the vigor and expense that has been poured into the battles against smoking, drinking, and illicit drug trafficking and use. We have erected a fine strong Maginot Line which protected one sector well enough, but meanwhile a mighty foe swept around the flank and overwhelmed us. Or, to pose another metaphor, sugar has been the elephant in the room while we of the CEWG have been listening ever so carefully for the gnawing of mice (heroin, speed, etc.) in the walls.

Why did Sugar Megadeath enjoy such success? I see seven contributing factors:

First, as the Michael Pollan quote on page 2 makes clear, for nearly all of us our slide into sugar addiction occurred so early in infancy that we have lost all memory of it. We can't remember before our third or fourth year, and by then we were already– think of the toddlers you know– engaged in a persistent daily mealtime struggle with our parents for *more of the sweet stuff, sooner!*

Second, this particular psychoactive substance is inextricably enmeshed with food, a necessity of life. Of all the other psychoactive substances, only alcohol comes close to playing such a central role, and only for a minority of us. Sugar meshes itself ever more into our meals– it may have been just for "dessert" a couple of generations ago, but now it has insinuated itself into all sorts of foods:

cereal, ketchup, McDonald's Big Macs, yogurt, granola, etc., etc. Sugar is in so much of our food that we consume great amounts without being aware of it.

Third, sugar is very important in the American farm economy. There are the sugarcane plantations of our subtropical states, and the sugarbeet farms of many other parts of the country, but above all there are the corn states of the Midwest. These last are now major players in the sugar trade thanks to the development, around 1970, of a blend of high-fructose corn syrup (HFCS) that has a taste and "mouthfeel" that most American consumers now *prefer* to cane sugar. To judge for yourself, do this: make yourself a glass of lemonade the old-fashioned way, with lemon juice, ice water, and cane sugar, then compare its taste to a chilled glass of Snapple "lemonade". Which do you prefer? Which do your *kids* prefer? Note that the Snapple is sweetened with HFCS. Now examine the labels of all the (processed) food items in your kitchen, and see how often you find HFCS listed. Don't overlook the Worcestershire sauce.

The attractiveness of HFCS to consumers has provided a vital market for the mountains of corn harvested annually in the Corn Belt. One out of every twelve bushels of corn is used to produced HFCS, and the U.S. is the world's lowest-cost producer of HFCS. HFCS is even less "natural" a food than cane sugar, and is now overwhelming human bodies which evolved fat-storage mechanisms over thousands of generations as hunter-gatherers– mechanisms that are totally unprepared to deal with HFCS.

Of course, the world as a whole has been on its way to sugar junkiedom for a long time. In the 130 years from the begining of the modern, post-slavery cane sugar economy to the advent of HFCS, i.e. from 1840 to 1970, world annual cane sugar production leapt from 830,000 tons to more than 70,000,000 tons. Thus the world increased its per-capita consumption of cane sugar some 20-fold *even before the glorious advent of HFCS!*

The fourth factor for the stealthy success of sugar has been the huge advertising effort on its behalf. American tastes had to be adapted to the ever-increasing portion of HFCS in its diet, but this was not difficult because of new products constantly being introduced to the market, along with their appealing mouthfeel and the clever supportive promotions *especially to children*. These promotions have ratcheted up our expectations of how sweet food is supposed to be. "A product is not deemed attractive if it is not as sweet as its competitor." Americans now consume an average 61 pounds of HFCS per year. Most of this takes the form of soft drinks, which the average American now drinks at the rate of 46 gallons per year. "Soft" and "fruit" drinks (and "milk" drinks such as Raging Cow) now account for 43% of all added sweeteners. Most of these added sweeteners are corn syrup products; we actually consume significantly *less* cane sugar and beet sugar than we did 40 years ago.

The fifth factor is that there has been essentially no criminal aspect in the marketing of sugar. By contrast, alcoholic beverages and tobacco products are tightly controlled and regulated, with minors especially well-protected against any access. Caffeine, if in the form of tea or coffee, is still considered an adult beverage, albeit without legal proscriptions against use by minors. Kids can get their caffeine in all sorts of soft drinks. But there are no barriers whatsoever to kids' access to sugar– actually, this drug is *preferentially* marketed to them, as a cursory inspection of the cereal aisle of a supermarket will demonstrate. Moreover, the food industry has taken note of the billion-dollar class action settlements against the tobacco companies: by 2005, their lobbying had led to passage in 20 states, and consideration in 11 more, of bills to prohibit lawsuits by people claiming a food company made them obese.

The sixth factor aiding sugar's quiet victory is that its bad health consequences are far in the future– or at least were until "adult onset" (Type 2) diabetes became an adolescent and even a childhood disease. It is only within the past decade that the public has made any clear connection between a sugar-drenched childhood and a diabetic adolescence.

Finally, there is that matter of *dose size*– the ideal marker of the great and terrible triumph of sugar in our times. Consider a drink of Coke. Sixty years ago, the typical individual portion ("dose size") was eight ounces in a pale green, hourglass-shaped bottle. Then came the 12-ounce cans, initially of steel and later of aluminum. Nowadays, paper/plastic cups or plastic bottles convey most of our "doses": the bottles are usually 16 ounces while the cups, at fast food joints, typically run from "medium" (16 ounces) through "large" (22 ounces) to "very large" or "big gulp" (32 ounces). There is no "small". The price structure strongly inclines one to choose the larger, for example the "extra large" might be priced at $1.99 and the "medium"at $1.59– twice as much sugar-rich beverage for only 25% more money. As if that weren't enough, some fast food outlets provide free refills. With even the 12-oz. cans giving the drinker– read the label– a 40-gram jolt of sugar, it's easy to see how a teenager can consume *half a pound* of sugar just by draining two "big gulps" per day. And that's just what happens: Americans now get a third of their sugar, and teenagers half of theirs, via soft drinks.

Now let's consider what a counterattack against HCFS, the most pernicious form of sugar, might look like:

They Took the Cocaine from Our Coke— Will They Now Take the HFCS from Our Food?

High-fructose corn syrup (HFCS) has become an enormous part of the American diet. To the extent that American health has gotten worse because of sugar's contribution to obesity, diabetes, etc., HFCS is a major part of that worsening.

In short, a dangerous substance has been insinuated into the American diet, and it's in our interest to see it removed. But we've been through this before: for the first 20 years of its commercial life, Coca-Cola® contained a modest quantity of cocaine. Concerns were raised, and the company eventually removed that psychoactive substance from its "stimulating elixir". There are some interesting parallels:

	Cocaine in Coca-Cola®	**HFCS in soft drinks**
Appearance on Market	1883	1973
Typical Dose ($1 in 2007)	5 milligrams	30 grams
Food Value	None	Minimal
Criminal Aspect	Minimal	None
Psychoactive Aspect	Stimulation, a "pick me up"	Sheer pleasure, a gladdening of spirit
Concerns Raised	1890s	1980s
Contribution to Mortality	c. 100/year	c. 100,000 year
Removed from Product(s)	1903	

This little illustration suggests that a counterattack against sugar, or at least that part of it consisting of HFCS, might be as easily won as that against the cocaine in soft drinks. But that's a very unlikely scenario; mighty forces of American capitalism will militate against there ever being a date like "2009" in the bottom right-hand corner of the above table. I foresee, rather, a long, arduous struggle very much in the model of the 40-year campaign against tobacco use. Tobacco enjoyed a long rise in popularity from the time of the mass production of cigarettes (1880s) until the first serious warnings from the Surgeon General (1964), followed by a decline by half in the following four decades.[2] We are now at the beginning of serious and sustained warnings about the dangers of excess sugar consumption, and we might expect that several decades will be needed to get sugar consumption back to where it was before the advent of HFCS. And meanwhile, what a swath of destruction of American bodies!

[2]Ironically, the decrease in smoking prevalence may have contributed to the obesity epidemic, since smokers tend to be leaner than nonsmokers.

Sugar is Sweet, and so is Hard Cold Cash

Start with a fact I may have mentioned before: This nation is in the middle of an epidemic of diabetes. One major reason for the epidemic is the growing rate of obesity among American citizens. One major reason for the obesity is the amount of carbohydrate-rich processed food eaten by Americans.

That would be your fast food, your chips in foil containers, your candy bars, your sugar water (often called "cola"), your sticky buns, your pizza– well, you know what it is. That stuff.

It's hugely profitable, that stuff. The people who sell it to you want you to eat more of it. When asked about their contribution to an epidemic, they say, "People have a choice." And of course, people do. But maybe, just in the spirit of *not killing their customers*, they might want to hold the line on the sugar and fat content of their foods.

But no. First there was "super-sizing," which is "why don't you have a lot more of this dreck for just a little more money so you'll think you're getting a deal, and we'll get pure profit." Swell idea. Too bad about your pancreas, kid, but have some more gunk.

Now showing up at your AMC theaters: the combo snack. Want to order a small popcorn? Well, you can, but it's darned hard. You have to insist. You're offered instead the "I Can Still See My Feet" combo or the "I Needed a New Glucometer Anyway" combo or the "I'm So Depressed I Want to Eat All Night" combo. I made those names up. But you can get a bucket of popcorn and a gallon of Coke and a Sugar Swizzle Treat that you need a Sherpa to help you carry to your seat, all for one low price. Low, comparatively speaking. Say: nine bucks.

I am not a purist. I understand how tempting those foods can be. I do not pretend that three pieces of lettuce and a small water make me feel cleansed and happy. I like that grease. But I also have diabetes, and it just ticks me off to see large corporations pandering to our most at-risk populations with ever more inventive stuff-your-face options.

We're here in the world capital of food disorders, where one half of the culture says, "You must be thin" and the other half says, "Eat, it'll make you happy," and there are lots of people made half crazy by that pounding dissonance.

Of course, "people have a choice." Right, like people have a choice whether or not to speak English. Culture is powerful. Culture is the air we breathe. In the mediasphere, the culture is so powerful that a "choice" to live another way is always difficult. If you're 13 and living with your parents and dealing with the social horrors of secondary education, making that "choice" may be close to impossible.

Maybe we should give those folks a little help rather than another burger. Maybe maximizing profit is not the only value.

Here's another thing: It costs the American taxpayers $2 billion a year to subsidize the sugar industry. Yup, we're paying for the stuff that's killing us. (Sugar is also killing the environment in the places where it's grown, but never mind that now.)

In 2000, sugar processors in default of loans dumped $400 million worth of sugar on the American government. It cost us $1 million a day just to store it. So do farmers have any incentive to switch over to another crop? Are you kidding? They're covered either way.

The health care costs of fighting diabetes are increasing exponentially. In essence, we pay at the pump and then we pay at the doctor's office. People may indeed have a choice, but the hidden costs of that choice are just astonishing. Plus, you know, pain and suffering and other non-quantifiable events. Kind of insane, isn't it?

--Jon Carroll
San Francisco Chronicle

II.

The Parable of the Penny Shot

Parable II.

The Ethanol Garden

The Ethanol Garden was created for Metro City's public inebriates: people who are inclined to get drunk every evening, but who lack the means or inclination to do so in private. The Garden is enclosed by high walls, within which is a large area partly under the open sky and partly sheltered. There are ample chairs, tables, toilets, storage lockers, and sleeping facilities.

Clients seeking admission to the Garden enter through the white north door. Only individuals previously registered as public inebriates may be admitted, and only by means of an electronic "handprint identifier" unique to each client. Clients may enter any time between 6 and midnight, but once inside must stay until the next morning.

The alcohol is dispensed as nearly-pure, 190-proof ethanol. It is available from 7 PM to shortly after midnight at a "bar" in the center of the Garden. Clients must pay cash for their ethanol, but it is provided by the Federal Government *tax-free* and *overhead-free*. That is, the only expense to the user is the actual cost of production of the ethanol: about $1.20 per gallon or one cent per ounce. Clients purchase their ethanol in ounce units, up to five ounces for a nickel; they rarely need more than 15 cents to cover their nightly "costs". Most clients prefer to dilute, and a variety of mixers– tasty, nutrient-rich fruit juice– are provided free for that purpose.

After the clients consume their desired quantity of alcohol, they make use of comfortable cots and blankets to sleep off their inebriation. This nightly client community polices itself quite nicely most of the time, even more so than traditional hobo communities. The Ethanol Garden has the advantage that shortages of alcohol, the major source of conflict among hoboes, never occur.

Clients may leave anytime between 8 and noon. A simple but hearty breakfast is available for those so desiring. Each departing client must make an important choice among three exits: the green south door, the golden east door, or the black west door. Each exit has a specific meaning and design, derived from Native American culture:

South Door (Green)	*"I will carry on as always"* A simple exit to the outside world.
West Door (Black)	*"I am sick, I need help"* A passageway, furnished with items of the undertaker's and gravedigger's crafts (coffins, winding cloths, headstones, etc.) leading to a clinic where minor ailments can be treated and major ones referred out.
East Door (Golden)	*"I've had enough of this life, I want to get sober"* A desk where the client is given a seven-day dose of Antabuse and enrolled in a 12-Step program, to the accompaniment of applause and cheering. Also, a counter where sets of clean clothes are available for free.

Once Metro City had its Ethanol Garden, the whole debilitating process of the inebriate's life— wandering about, begging, purchasing booze, consuming in public, passing out in public, being taken to the drunk tank– was brought under one roof and transmuted into a far pleasanter experience for all. There was immediate relief from most of the nuisances of public inebriation. Just one such nuisance, "begging for booze money", was so noxious that its amelioration promptly commended the Garden to the public.

Of course, there was a clandestine, "hiding away" aspect in creating this walled garden– but interested citizens found they could learn about its goings-on through vivid newspaper and television reportage. Citizens and clients alike appreciated the frankness and directness of the pricing scheme which showed that alcohol is, in fact, ridiculously *cheap*. Also, the rich symbolism of each morning's exit– choosing among the three doors– gave an epic quality to the inebriate's life and reminded him that he has some control over his path in the grand scheme of life. Each morning, he chooses either to continue as before, to acknowledge passively that alcohol is slowly poisoning his body and hastening his death, or to seize the hope for a Recovered life.

The Lessons of the Ethanol Garden

The Ethanol Garden should be regarded as a "thought experiment" which just might expose three great fallacies about public inebriation:

Fallacy One: "Booze is expensive." No way! Booze is dirt cheap; it's the flavoring, packaging, wholesaling, retailing, advertising, taxes, and other puffery and exploitation that turns a pennyworth of ethanol into a five-dollar vodka cocktail.

Fallacy Two: "Boozers can't help it." Maybe in past decades they were helpless, but not any longer– not in the age of Antabuse and Alcoholics Anonymous. Millions of "boozers" of all sorts choose every day to be sober.

Fallacy Three: "A community of boozers can't govern itself." Maybe not in the long run, but good governance only needed to last the night's bout. Once the few real needs– safety, shelter, warmth, food– were abundantly supplied, governance took care of itself, and supplies could be replenished in the afternoon. (It proved wise, nonetheless, to have separate Gardens for men and women. It also proved wise to check weapons at the door– and to lend out musical instruments freely.)

If Ethanol Gardens are successfully established in this country, they might easily expose a fourth fallacy: that we must resign ourselves, year after year, decade after decade, generation after generation, to all the nasty aspects of public inebriation. And that's the whole point of the above Parable: the notion of replacing *nastiness* with *decency*. We do best when we regard substance users as human beings and approach them with kindness.

Of course, public inebriation is an extreme form of the vast world of alcohol consumption. There are other extreme and dysfunctional manifestations: drunken binges, alcohol-fueled violence, liver disease, and traffic accidents. In spite of these nasty aspects, the overwhelming impact of alcohol— at least in the Western world– is positive. Beer, cocktails, and especially wine have contributed immensely to the "social goods" of modern society. For the essential human need of stress relief and "attitude adjustment", alcohol has become supremely well adapted and enjoys literally hundreds of millons of safe, judicious, and well controlled "dosings" each day.

A Brief History of Alcohol in the Western World

Ethyl alcohol is one of the natural and inevitable products of organic fermentation. Literally hundreds of the foods humans have learned to eat– corn, rye, berries, potatoes, grapes, peaches, rice, milk– will begin to ferment if in a reasonably warm, moist environment. Usually all that's needed is a little yeast, which may simply blow in from the organic environment.

It appears that this miracle of alcohol fermentation was discovered independently on dozens– perhaps hundreds– of occasions in early human history. Hunter-gatherers no doubt found that certain overripe fruits may have lacked in sweetness but had pleasant qualities of a different sort. At a later stage of human development, early agriculturists in the Fertile Crescent, the Indus Valley, eastern China, and Middle America created an improved environment for these friendly yeasts: fixed abodes with storage of cultivated or gathered foodstuffs. The technical challenge, then as now, was to refine the fermentation process so as to minimize the nastier-tasting byproducts of a "controlled rotting".

The result, after generations of trial and error, was a gamut of fermented drinks, all of great antiquity: beer, ale, wine, kumass, mead, et cetera. All of them, by virtue of their ethyl alcohol, provided their consumers with the wonderful psychoactive effects (see page 3) of *comfort, relief from pain*, and *"attitude adjustment"*. Paeans of thanks for these drinks have been spoken and sung, on six continents, for millenia– such as this from Ecclesiates 31:

Wine gives life if drunk in moderation
What is life without wine?
It came into being to make people happy.
Drunk at the right time and in the right amount,
wine makes for a glad heart and a cheerful mind.

Or the Symposia of Classical Greece where, it was averred, every serious subject should be discussed twice: once while sober, and once while wine-drunk.

Until about 400 years ago, almost all the world's alcohol beverages were perforce mild, for a simple reason: fermentation only can yield a maximum of 14% ethyl alcohol content because the helpful yeast are killed at that level. A few drinkers in northern climes found that the right kind of freezing could increase the alcohol content of the residual liquid (think applejack), but for the most part the world awaited the breakthrough of distillation.

Consumption of alcohol in America has undergone five distinct phases, as illuminated by these data on per capita consumption by Americans over age 14:

Year	Beer	Wine	Spirits	TOTAL
1770	~0.05	~0.05	~3.80	~3.90
1850	0.14	0.08	1.88	2.10
1860	0.27	0.10	2.16	2.53
1870	0.44	0.10	1.53	2.07
1871-1880	0.56	0.14	1.02	1.72
1881-1890	0.90	0.14	0.95	1.99

1891-1900	1.18	0.11	0.86	2.15
1901-1910	1.39	0.15	0.96	2.50
1911-1915	1.48	0.14	0.94	2.56
1916-1919	1.08	0.12	0.76	1.96
1920-1933	(Prohibition-- no reliable data)			
1940	0.73	0.16	0.67	1.56
1950	1.04	0.23	0.77	2.04
1960	0.99	0.22	0.86	2.07
1970	1.14	0.27	1.11	2.52
1980	1.38	0.34	1.04	2.76
1990	1.34	0.33	0.77	2.45
2000	1.22	0.31	0.65	2.18

(Source: National Institute on Alcohol Abuse and Alcoholism. Amounts expressed as gallons of pure ethanol equivalent per capita per year)

In the later Colonial era, more than 90% of Americans lived on farms which were largely self-sufficient in food–and in homemade whiskey. This was the zenith of American ethanol consumption, at about four gallons per adult per year, or the equivalent of two cocktails every day.

Regulation and taxation suppressed much of this home-based industry in the early days of the Republic, as did the early manifestations of the Temperance Movement. Commercial production and distribution of distilled spirits (particularly whiskey) led to a second peak of ethanol consumption just before the Civil War. Not evident in the above data is the *real* blessing of Johnny Appleseed, who augmented the ability of Midwestern farmers to grow apples not just for pies but for *applejack*. "The sweetest fruit makes the strongest drink, and in the north, where grapes didn't do well, that was usually the apple. Up until

Prohibition, an apple grown in America was far less likely to be eaten than to wind up in a barrel of [hard] cider." (Michael Pollan, *The Botany of Desire*)

After the Civil War, great improvements in the mass production by breweries– and the cultural impact of Irish and German immigrants– resulted in beer gradually supplanting spirits as the alcoholic intoxicant of choice. Thus a third peak of ethanol consumption was attained in the decade before America's entry into the First World War.

The "noble experiment" of Prohibition (1920-1933) ensued. To judge from liver cirrhosis data, per capita consumption fell signficantly, but at the cost of respect for the law as millions of Americans cheerfully slipped into speakeasies and other venues of illicit substance use.

A fourth peak in per-capita consumption was reached in 1980, with beer and spirits roughly as popular as in the 1911-1915 peak. By then wine was at last playing a major role, but still only averaging barely one glass per week per person. This peak was followed by yet another era of temperance, this time taking the form of "light" beverages, stringent enforcement of DUI laws, and decreased inclination to imbibe at lunchtime.

The Business of Booze

I know something about the ancient and honorable wine business, by virtue of being a grapegrower and winemaker (see pages 86-87). I learnt the stunning central truth about this business some 40 years ago, when I discovered that drinkable California wine ("Red Mountain") could be had for a dollar a *gallon*. What a concept, that one could be gloriously drunk for two bits! That basic price has of course gone up since then thanks mostly to inflation, but I note that drinkable Cabernet can still be had on the bulk market for $6 per gallon. That still gives a reasonable return to the grapegrower out in California's Central Valley, who can get eight tons to the acre from his machine-tended, machine-harvested fruit, and can produce perhaps 1,200 gallons of wine from those eight tons. I've watched eight-ton batches being brought in, crushed, fermented, and pressed out: in 10 days the raw wine is ready, sitting up there in a stainless-steel tank about the size of a panel truck. It's quite satisfying to think that those 1,200 gallons are worth $7,200 on the bulk market, and more– MUCH more– if the quality of the wine will bear a certain amount of puffery:

Patriotic Ethanol

A few years ago Congress passed a measure aimed at an annual purchase of five billion gallons of ethanol, for use in the nation's vehicle fuels. This ethanol is to come from the excess corn and other ethanol sources of Midwestern farms. The farms, some of them huge corporate enterprises, are to be "preferred raw material sources"– i.e., Brazilian ethanol producers need not apply.

If we have "preferred raw material sources", it's just a short step to "preferred finished product sources". I propose the creation of a new vodka company, "American Eagle", which alone will be permitted to buy some of that Midwestern ethanol. The company will make two brands, Regular and Premium. "Regular" will have a basic package (plastic bottle, one-color label), almost no marketing or advertising outreach, and distribution to discount outlets such as Costco or K-Mart. "Premium" will have a fancy package (cut-glass bottle, four-color label with gold leaf, bronze cap), extravagant marketing and advertising, and distribution to upscale outlets such as Whole Foods.

Costs of the two brands will be as follows, per 750-ml. fifth (ethanol will be purchased from the Midwestern supplies at the prevailing price of $1.50/gallon, and Mountain Spring Water for the Premium brand at $.30/gallon):

	American Eagle Vodka (80 proof)	American Eagle Premium Vodka (100 proof)
Ethanol	$0.12 (.08 gallon)	$0.15 (.10 gallon)
Water	0 (.12 gallon)	$0.03 (.10 gallon)
Packaging	$0.06	$1.00

Advertising	$0.04	$1.00
Distribution	$0.30	$0.50
Retailer share	$1.00	$2.00
Retail price	$6.00	$12.00
Profit	$4.48	$7.32

American Eagle vodka will compete smartly against imported brands, quickly achieving market dominance by its attractive price and patriotic evocations. A feasible target will be annual sales of 600 million fifths, or a 75% market share of American vodka sales. This will yield annual "profits" of more than $3 billion, all of which will be forwarded to a noble international cause. All this will require only about 50 million gallons of ethanol– just **1% of that Midwestern production.**

Some Americans have the quaint belief that they can distinguish among premium vodkas. Of course this is nonsense, as all vodka (from Russian *voda*, water + *'khol*, alcohol) is identical, so long as the ethanol distillation is clean and the water reasonably pure. A series of well-publicized double-blind tastings among upscale vodkas (Absolut, Grey Goose, Ketel One, American Eagle Premium, etc.) will demonstrate that tasters cannot reliably determine which is which, and so might as well buy the cheapest. Then vodka can be put in its proper place in the connoisseurship of distilled liquors.

American Eagle retail outlets will be exempted from Federal excise taxes, State excise taxes, sales taxes, BATF reports, and other tiresome paperwork. They would simply subtract end-of-month inventory from start-of-month inventory, multiply by $4.48 (or $7.32), and send in a check to "U.S. Treasury– Africa AIDS

Fund". This money would more than double our contribution to that continent's struggle against AIDS, thus further burnishing America's reputation abroad.

In the years to come, American vodka lovers could take trips to southern Africa with the money saved by choosing American Eagle. They could visit villages in Mozambique where grateful survivors of the AIDS plague will have erected shrines to the Blessed Virgin fashioned entirely from American Eagle Premium vodka bottles, and shrines to George Bush fashioned from the Regular vodka bottles.

"Patriotic Ethanol" jests about taking the taxes from vodka sales and sending them directly to Africa to help its AIDS problem. But seriously, folks: experience shows us that alcohol drinkers are *quite willing to bear a very big surcharge* of costs on their favored drug. As with sugar and most other psychoactive substances, the best approach– politically, morally, economically– is to tax the thing sufficiently so that the commonwealth can cover all the downstream costs of usage, and then some. My rough guess of "sufficient tax" is $120 per gallon of pure alcohol, which works out to about $12 per quart of whisky, $3 per six-pack of beer, and also $3 per fifth of wine. This tax would put enormous selective pressure in favor of the good stuff: my excellent Pinot Noir would rise from about $22 to $25 (+14%) per retail bottle, while the cheapest plonk would rise from $2 to $5 (+150%). Likewise, Chivas Regal scotch would go from about $30 to $40 (+33%) per fifth, while Old Rotgut would rise from $9 to $19 (+111%). Americans would drink less of the cheap stuff (fewer hangovers!) and probably less overall. If consumption of pure alcohol declined to 2.0 gallons per person per year, the overall tax revenue would be about $72 billion per year. That should cover most or all of the costs of cirrhosis treatment, drunk tanks, DUI mayhem, etc.– and maybe leave enough to fund prevention education programs for youth.

III.

The Parable of Good Junk

Parable III.

Thirteen Reasons Why Heroin is Good for America

(Herewith the closing arguments of Defense Attorney Jack Hibbert, in the penalty phase of the trial of Mr. Shaquille Jones, convicted of selling heroin to his neighbors in East Oakland.)

"Ladies and gentlemen of the jury, I urge you to show compassion in this case. It may be true that Mr. Jones has had a small part in commerce which certainly has its harmful side. But this same commerce also has aspects which in fact strengthen and improve our society. Let me enumerate the many ways whereby heroin is good for America."

(Addressing his comments to Juror #1, a middle-aged White executive) "Heroin is a growth industry. Junkie-oriented clinics, rehabilitation centers, methadone-maintenance programs, police narcotics bureaus, and government funding agencies have all enjoyed a great expansion. Many people now earn a good living– legally– off of the heroin epidemic. Professional unemployment is down, and more inner-city office space is being used."

(Turning to Juror #2, a Society columnist for the Oakland Tribune) "We have a few new entrants into America's upper class. Perhaps 10 or 20 families or groups of individuals have made enormous fortunes in recent years from heroin trafficking. These top-level connections and importers are adding a little diversity and color to our upper crust."

(To Juror #3, a 27-year old unemployed Black man) "Some of the billions of dollars resulting from the purchases of American junkies is trickling down to the lower levels of the trafficking system. Many small-time connections, couriers, protection men, and laboratory operators have gotten out with sizable profits. And of course the opium farmers of Asia and Latin America continue to reap enough profits from their cash crops to lead decent lives."

(To Juror #4, a young White Berkeley-trained psychologist) "Junkies provide a superb training ground for aspiring clinicians and social workers. Junkies are the acid test: if you can succeed with them, you can succeed with anyone."

(Turning to Juror #5, an elderly Black grandmother, sole provider for a family of five) "Junkies help redistribute the wealth. The goods they steal from stores and homes are made available to poor people at bargain prices. In some cases, they will even 'steal to order' for customers. This means that poor people can afford a better lifestyle than if they had to pay full price for their consumables."

(With a sly nod to Juror #6, a 54-year-old businessman) "Heroin makes people calm, passive, and unambitious. A lot of people who would otherwise be fomenting revolution, or committing acts of violence, or competing with the rest of us for good jobs, are not doing so because they're strung out. Also, because male junkies are largely impotent, they are not competing with other men for the scarce resource of the sexual favors of women."

(To Juror #7, an intense young White man with a penchant for reading Ayn Rand during breaks) "The birth rate among female junkies is far lower than among other

women of similar age and social class. In addition, the mortality rate among the babies of junkies is very high. Thus, junkies are doing their part to ameliorate the population problem."

(To Juror #8, an Asian-American graduate student) "Heroin gives severely disturbed people a way of coping with the world. These people, without opiation, would simply cave in under the anxiety and confusion of it all; they would then have to be cared for by public institutions. Their self-motivated hustle for junk organizes their lives and quiets their pain."

(With a sympathetic smile to Juror #9, a twentysomething White man in his 3rd year of community college.) "Junkies give the rest of us a clear idea of what not to be. In a complicated world, it is often hard for an adolescent to develop an identity. This task is made easier by the existence of the American junkie: one simply tries to be the opposite of everything that this most despised of citizens is."

(To Juror #10, a young gay Latino) "Heroin addicts make great scapegoats. They can take the blame for a lot of social ills, blame which otherwise might fall upon us. They can be scapegoated and will not fight back nor attempt to refute the accusations of wickedness levelled against them. They serve as the butt of much inner-city humor, rather like the village fool of medieval English tradition."

(To Juror #11, a middle-aged Black man) "Junk integrates the races. Only among drunks and junkies do we see such a degree of easy social interaction among White, Black, Latino, and Asian. The junkie sees clearly that The Drug

transcends trivial issues of ethnic or cultural differences. This comradeship at the bottom of the social barrel serves as an inspiration to the rest of us."

(To Juror #12, a 52-year-old Latino writer and journalist) "Thirty or 40 years on heroin ages a person in an extraordinary way. No other class of Americans, except Skid Row drunks, undergoes the atrocious day-to-day wear on body and soul that the American junkie experiences. Those who survive several decades of this kind of life show the scars of it, with faces and bodies wizened by a hard long road. These tough old birds show us how to survive with character."

"And finally, ladies and gentlemen of the jury, we must recognize that heroin makes us confront the ultimate cop-out. The American junkie is so persistent and indefatigable in his pursuit of the fix that we are forced to wonder, 'maybe they're on to something.' We are forced into a self-examination of our own needs for the junk nirvana, for complete detachment and painlessness, for a self-indulgent yielding up of all the struggle and changefulness of our lives. We are forced to realize the dull, heroin-like quality of many of our 'straight' indulgences: television, alcohol, banal sentiments, procrastination, plastic tastes. Perhaps we end by realizing that junk– in *all* its form s – is a critical impediment to the further development of our civilization, and that if we can overcome it in our lives we can genuinely hope that human social evolution will make a great leap forward."

"For all these reasons, ladies and gentlemen of the jury, I urge your compassion and understanding as you decide upon the fate of young Mr. Jones."

The IDU Epidemic Summarized

For the first 11 years of my work at the Haight-Ashbury Free Clinics, I focused mostly on gauging the impacts of drug use and devising the most cost-effective ways to ameliorate those impacts. The major (illicit) drug in those days was heroin, with cocaine, speed, and downers playing minor roles. Most of the impacts had to do with disruption of people's work and home life. There were medical aspects as well: abscesses, hepatitis-B, and the occasional life-threatening overdose. But mortality was low– less than 1% per year even among heroin users– and we kept seeing the same people year after year.

All this changed in February 1983, with the visit of Andrew Moss to our Clinic. Dr. Moss warned that a "gay-related immune disorder", highly fatal, would inevitably spread to the IDUs who were a big part of HAFC's clientele. That Spring and Summer, I attended meetings of a San Francisco Department of Public Health committee monitoring this new infectious disease. Month after month, we heard disquieting reports of swift increases in the city's caseload. However, it wasn't until September that we heard about the first heterosexual IDU case.

Twenty-two years later I found myself thinking the endgame might be near. The SFDPH reported only 38 AIDS cases of heterosexual IDUs in 2004, down from a peak of 225 cases in 1992. All our prevention effort s – "street-level" education, bleach distribution, needle exchange, cocktail therapies, prevention case management– seem to have come together into a "virtuous circle" of contagion control. The rate of new IDU cases looks as if it will go even lower. Moreover, the City has been spared what we most feared in the early days: a "secondary spread" of HIV disease from heterosexual IDUs to their non-IDU sexual partners and their children.

Is it time for asumming up of the AIDS epidemic among S.F.'s IDUs? Not quite yet: there are real risks of a resurgence of infection among younger injectors, especially those in the speed scene. However, we can imagine that the first portion of that summing up might read like this:

HIV arrived in San Francisco's straight IDU population around 1981. The virus, unnoticed, spread rapidly. By the fall of 1983, when the first actual AIDS case was diagnosed, some 300 IDUs were infected. The number of infected went up fast, to about 600 by the end of 1984, 900 by the end of 1985, and 1,300 by the end of 1986. During 1986 and 1987 effective public health campaigns, mostly bleach outreach at first, were launched and contagion decelerated. By the late 1990s the infection rate of straight IDUs was down to about 120 per year. The reporting of actual IDU AIDS cases reflected this infection curve with a lag time of about six years. There were 23 new cases in 1986, 52 in 1988, 121 in 1990, and 225 in 1992; thereafter there was a decline, to 144 new cases in 1996, 89 in 2000, and 38 in 2004. This has been a classic epidemic, with infection peaking in 1986, disease diagnoses in 1992, and deaths in 1994.

Twenty-five Years of AIDS and IDUs

It is now (2007) 25 years since AIDS first came to the attention of the world. Let's take a look at how the situation in San Francisco changed over that quarter-century:

- The heroin-using population was *barely half* the size it is now. My "period prevalence" estimate was that, in 1980, about 7,000 San Franciscans used heroin on more than an occasional basis. My estimate for 2007 is that there are 12,000 such users.

• Heroin users were younger then: the median age in 1981 was just under 30, whereas now it's about 40. The gender and ethnic distribution was much the same then as now: two-thirds male, about 55% White, 25% Black, 15% Hispanic, and 5% Asian.

• The real cost of heroin was about *eight times* what it is now. The 1981 buyer paid about $3.50 per pure milligram of street heroin (correcting for inflation, $8.00 in today's dollars.) The 2007 buyer pays only about $1.00 for a pure milligram. "Bags" of heroin, in 2005 as in 1981, may weigh the same and cost the same, but the stuff is more likely to be 10% rather than 5% pure.

• Then as now, most S.F. junkies inject. Back in 1981, 95% of heroin users treated at the Haight-Ashbury Free Clinic preferred to inject. A quarter-century later– despite AIDS, despite heroin's low price– injection is still the preferred route for 90% of users.

• Partly as a result of the weakness of 1981's heroin, people overdosed far less often. Emergency room mentions of various drugs have been reported to the nationwide Drug Abuse Warning Network system for 20 years. In the early 80s, there were 200 mentions of heroin/morphine from the San Francisco Bay Area in a typical year; in the early years of the new century, there were more than 2,000 per year.

• Heroin users died less often, too. The S.F. medical examiner reported only nine deaths due to heroin in 1981, compared to an average of 120 per year during 2000-2002.

• In my 1981 report, I recounted the recent history of speed in San Francisco: a huge surge of abuse during 1967-1971, which then almost vanished during the mid-1970s, then a resurgence beginning in 1979. "Street observations disclose a continued increase of speed among gays," I wrote, "also a strong surge in popularity among the New Wave or 'punk' subculture, and an increased preference for the intravenous or intranasal route as opposed to the oral route." The timing could not have been worse: a surge of speed injection among gay men just when HIV was spreading widely– and silently– among them.

A Pyrrhic Defeat?

This is frustrating. A quarter-century of the AIDS epidemic, a quarter-century of the "war on drugs", a quarter-century of hard work by HAFC and a dozen other well-run programs to get people off heroin– and there are more users than ever, and the drug is cheaper than ever. It seems as if neither a deadly disease, nor vigorous law enforcement, nor sincere and diligent treatment efforts, have stemmed the tide of heroin in the City– or even diverted many people away from injection and toward safer routes. We've been defeated big time.

Or have we? Our defeat may have been Pyrrhic in the sense that we can say, "one more defeat like that and we've won the war!" Here's why:

• There's much less property crime. Reported burglaries in the City, for example, dropped from 17,700 in 1981 to 7,050 in 2004. Perhaps because heroin is so much cheaper people don't need to steal so much.

• Harm reduction, as a means of slowing HIV contagion, has really worked. The seroconversion rate of the City's IDUs is estimated (2006) at 0.5% per year. Newly-infected IDUs barely replace the infected IDUs who die, so overall prevalence holds steady at 10% or so. Meanwhile, physician prescription of methadone is under serious consideration; in this age of HIV, I regard methadone as the best harm reduction of all.

The Future of Analgesia

Pyrrhic Defeat embodies two marvelous lessons. Firstly, prohibition simply won't work when it comes to analgesia: people *will have* whatever works to give them solace from pain. People can be indefatigable toward that end– cunning, manipulative, persistent, ruthless, stunningly creative– and all the more so if their pain is profound (as from spinal cord injury or kidney stones) or multifaceted (physical + psychological + emotional). For milder pain, such as the vexation and irritability at the end of a hard workday, people *will have* a milder forms of analgesic such as a martini. To try to prohibit this is to court frustration and defeat.

The second lesson is that Defeat has a bright side. The sheer strength of market forces has done its work for all the substances, legal and illegal, which address the human need for "comfort, relief from pain, attitude adjustment" (see p. 3). For example:

• There are now at least four major sources of heroin for the American and European markets: Mexico, northern South America, Southeast Asia (especially the Golden Triangle centered on northern Burma), and Southwest Asia (especially Afghanistan). The mass of heroin needed to supply these markets is minuscule compared to the total mass of imported goods– for the U.S., annually, perhaps 10 tons of heroin among 400,000,000 tons of imported goods– so the challenge of smuggling is not great. The result is that plenty of heroin gets to users, from a variety of sources whose competition drives prices down. The result of *that* is that property crimes "to support junkie habits" are declining even as the number of junkies increases.

• Alcohol has obtained a secure place in our society; there are no serious attempts to revive Prohibition. If anything, this substance is even more an unremarkable part of daily life than a generation ago, thanks partly to the wider role of wine as a beverage. A variety of regulations set reasonable boundaries on the availability and use of alcohol. Taxation covers the cost of this regulation with money to spare; government could probably get a far larger chunk of the American alcohol dollar if it wanted, as was suggested in the Parable of Section II.

• In the middle between mild alcohol and mighty heroin are the narcotic analgesics, particularly hydrocodone (Vicodin®) and oxycodone (OxyContin®) which are rapidly rising in popularity. Just in the seven years from 1995 to 2002, Drug Abuse Warning Network reports of hydrocodone misuse rose by 160% and those of oxycodone by 560%. By 2005, more than 7% of Americans sampled in the National Survey on Drug Use and Health reported *non-medical* use of hydrocodone. Moreover, the National Survey on Drug Use and Health found that the proportion of youth aged 12 to 17 reporting ever misusing prescription pain relievers rose from 1.2% in 1989 to 11.4% in 2004. These analgesics are America's legal, middle-class, respectable morphine, prescribed for a wide range of complaints. The unused portions of those tens of millions of prescriptions sit in the medicine cabinets, in their little brown plastic bottles, awaiting use at other times when solace from some sort of pain is desired.

A personal note here: three times in my life, I've suffered from kidney stones. I can testify that those experiences were the most extraordinary pain I have ever experienced: excruciating, overwhelming, life-ablating, maximal pain, 12 on a scale of 10. Each time– thanks be to Providence!– I was able to ingest an opiate analgesic (Percodan or oxycodone) after two or three hours of misery. What a wonderful, steep gradient from hell to solace! Within 10 minutes, all was well; I "knew" the pain was still there, but it simply didn't matter. Then I could undertake the simple cure of flushing my system with a gallon of water a day until "the stones passed".

The experience was like a religious conversion. In a profound way, I came to Believe in Pain, and I came to regard the opiate as a Manifestation of Providence. There was an absolutist aspect to this: *absolutely* I want such effective analgesia to be quickly available for any human being who has to face such pain, *absolutely* I will give preference to relief from pain over fear of addiction. And I credit *psychological* or *emotional* pain as quite capable of reaching the same excruciating heights as *physical* pain.

Which led me to wonder– how much of America feels as I do on this matter? Surely any person who's had kidney stones, and any woman who's gone through childbirth, plus the huge numbers who've experienced severe psychological or emotional pain. I daresay We Who Stand in Awe of Pain constitute a majority– and if so, we are in a position to demand and get sensible policies for pain drugs.

IV.

The Parable of Switched Uppers

Parable IV.

A Reverie on Cultural Buffers

It had been a long afternoon.

Tom English, the Newark representative to the National Drug Epidemiology Group, leaned back resignedly in his chair as the lights went up. The man from DEA has just finished his slide presentation. Tom had seen it all before: "The DEA World Strategy for Caffeine Interdiction and Eradication". There were the familiar charts, tables, and maps, showing the annual flow into the U.S. of 8,000 kilos of high-purity Southwest Asian caffeine, 6,000 of Southeast Asian, and 3,000 of "Mexican Brown", that old "caffhead" favorite with its strong burnt-nut aroma. Tom had listened to the man tout the same methods that had failed so many generations of DEA agents before: the fast boats with their sophisticated weaponry (did they think the smugglers would try to dash toward our coast flying "Dare you to catch me!" signal flags?), the "caff-sniffing" German Shepherds (hadn't these guys even *heard* of vacuum sealing?), the tired old agency-cooperation diagrams with all those arrows and dashed lines (as if *any* of those Saudi, or Burmese, or Mexican bureaucrats weren't already on the take from the caffeine lords!) As always with the DEA, Tom felt the urge to ask impertinent questions. But this guy had particularly irritated him– he had had to repress an impulse to run in front of the screen, blocking the image of the new YOBAN-80 satellite infrared detection system for coffee plants, waving his arms, and screaming, "You idiot! You guys spend all that money on high-tech junk and now there are more caff addicts than ever!" Instead he had fumed quietly about how caffeine had destroyed his beloved Newark in such a short time. While the Feds and the State had pissed away the taxpayers' dollars in useless efforts to interdict the flood of imported caffeine, downtown had become devastated– a dangerous place to go even in broad daylight– nearly 100% Irish now, more than 70% of them unemployed, half the families on welfare– all the great jazz places closed or moved to the suburbs, replaced by seedy bars with names like "Blarney Stone", reeking of cheap whiskey and stale beer– and always the danger of unprovoked assault by caffed-out freaks.

Now the DEA man was droning on about "the new White House initiatives". Tom sighed wearily and mused on how he had seen them come and he had seen them go, these White Houses. The Reagan Administration ("we declare a total War on Drugs"). Bush *pére* ("read my lips, you merchants of caffeine death: you...are...history!") The Clinton crew ("our young people are our most precious resource"). And now the Bush *fils* team taking its turn trying to convert platitudes into policy ("from now on, Zero Tolerance for drug use of any sort").

The morning session had been so much better, thought Tom. There were the regional city summaries with their usual clarity– the NDEG could now declare that caffeine abuse prevalence was up everywhere, while heroin was down, speed was down in the Northeast but not anywhere else, and PCP was making a comeback in the West. All the city representatives had agreed that caffeine abuse was their #1 drug problem and that the abusers were increasingly smoking "black" caffeine– the sulfide form, with its 90% to 95% purity– rather than snorting or injecting the hydrochloride form of the drug, which was only 30% to 60% pure. Then there was Ziv Ben-Rutter's excellent report on the status of street chemistry methods for preparing "black"– a third technology, involving use of those new Japanese home freeze-drying machines, had now emerged to join the well-known ether-and-egg-whites and ammonia-and-Drano methods. Ben-Rutter had passed around samples of those little black "rocks" (which every literate American could now recognize thanks to all those *Time* and *Newsweek* cover stories) and had explained how the three home-chemistry methods led to subtle variations in the patina and texture of the "rocks".

The final morning speaker, Dr. Mohammed Bin-Ardo, had been best of all. He had described the impact of caffeine on Asian economies and societies– how the "Medina cartel" was corrupting government after government in the Arabian peninsula, how illicit caffeine exports were even exceeding oil as a revenue source for Persian Gulf countries, how this drug money was being laundered in Beirut and Singapore and Hong Kong, how there was an acceleration in emigration to the U.S. of educated Arabs fleeing their corrupt and increasingly violent countries, and how thousands of small-scale highland Burmese farmers had learned to conceal their tea plants in the outlying parts of the old British coca plantations.

John McAllister, the San Diego representative, had asked Dr. Bin-Ardo if the trade in high-purity caffeine had affected the traditional coffee-drinking patterns of the Yemen villages. Dr. Bin-Ardo had replied that these patterns had not changed and further, that there had been a puzzling absence of adverse reactions to caffeine reported by Yemeni emergency rooms. Bin-Ardo speculated that some sort of "cultural buffer" was working, such as that which kept immigrants to the American West relatively sober on beer and wine while the Indians got drunk and crazy on whisky. This had provoked another of John's discourses, this one on the possibility that the Western world "might prefer its caffeine to be weak, legal, and part of everyday social life rather than strong, illicit, and part of deviant subcultures like now". McAllister's suggestion had made the NDEG group nervous– imagine a whole country hooked on caffeine!– and Tom had chuckled inwardly at the hilarious image of hardened Third Ward Irish caffheads squatting in their "black" houses sipping coffee like so many Yemeni tribesmen. But Tom enjoyed the ideas this somewhat eccentric Californian triggered in his own imagination. He pondered some "what-ifs": what if that 17th-Century sultan hadn't suppressed coffee drinking in the Ottoman Empire? What if the British had gotten the Chinese addicted to tea rather than opium in the early 1800's? And what if the British had made all those millions of Irish indentured servants chew on tea leaves, rather than coca leaves, to keep their energies up as they did the Empire's hard work?

Tom's attention returned to the present. The Fed's talk seemed finally to be winding up, thank God. What a waste of time! Why couldn't we have had another field trip into the clean December New Orleans air?, he wondered. Yesterday's outing to the Desist Projects had been such an eye-opener. They had walked among the half-ruined project buildings and the pathetic remnants of gardens and playgrounds. Tom wondered if any of the skinny redheaded kids he saw had much of a future. "Black" had settled over the Desist Projects like an evil pall– empty apartments had been looted of every item of fixtures to pay for habits, and there was an average of one killing per week, plus gunfire nearly every night. As if that weren't enough, there were reports that the L.A. gangs were moving in. Tom knew them well from the news reports: the Skins and the Phlegms, with their distinctive pink or white bandannas, all of them ambitious, ruthless White toughs who wouldn't hesitate to kill to secure dominance of a "black" market. The "Pacific Palisades set" and the "Mulholland Drive boys"– or perhaps some local admirers– had already left their distinctive graffiti on brick walls of the Projects.

Tom suddenly felt drowsy. He regretted having stayed out so very late last night, exploring all those dives in the riotous company of the Chicago and Denver representatives. They had ended the night at the Caké du Monde, savoring hot beignets and steaming cups of dark green cokee. Altogether too little sleep– he fought the urge to doze.

Just then there was a rattling of cups at the door. Ah! It was the waiter wheeling in the refreshements for the afternoon cokee break. The Royal Orleans (splendid establishment!) was offering a fine range of brews– exquisite indigo Burmese– the familiar pea-green Peruvian, rich and strong, he could smell its invigorating aroma already– a smaller pot of Sanko ("97% cocaine-free")– handsome silver bowls for the sugar and lime– packs of La Paz and Sherlock Holmes brands of chewing gum– then the coca drinks sitting in their big bowls of ice: Classic Coke, Diet Coke, Pepsi Coca, Lima Lime, Cuzco Coca. Tom's spirits perked up.

The sight of the Classic Coke with its blue-and-white logo (famous the world over) put Tom in mind of what Dr. Ben-Rutter had told him. Apparently all the rumors Tom had heard over the years were true: the original Coke had *actually contained a small quantity of caffeine!* That explained those turn-of-the-century ads for Coca Cola, with the photos of generals, opera singers, Senators, even a *pope*, all praising it as such a fine "stimulant elixir". No *wonder* they liked it so much– they were nothing but caffheads, those prim Victorians! Of course the FDA had clamped down in 1903, so history was history. But maybe, just maybe, John McAllister was onto something– what if we gave caffeine abusing clients some sort of prescription cola drink, maybe a Tang flavor, under careful physician supervision of course– maybe they could get used to taking their caffeine in this mild, legalized form, and, like those Victorians, keep out of trouble. With the right kind of public education and social support, we could perhaps create a "cultural buffer" against caffeine abuse just as in the case of... of...

Mick's voice interrupted Tom's reverie. "Okay, let's take a 20-minute break– please try to be back by 4:00." It was time for afternoon cokee– Tom decided he'd have a cup, well maybe two, to perk up his spirits for the remaining session– but he *would* be sure to drink decoke after dinner so he wouldn't be jittery or restless later in the evening.

Tom hesitated before heading for the table– as a well-socialized American adult, he subconsciously avoided an unseemly display of haste when approaching the morning or afternoon cokee break. Presently he was part of a cheerful throng advancing upon the table. Cups clanked, the fizz of cola sounded, gum-wrappers ripped, and their was a soft ripple of laughter. The room was soon abuzz with the animated conversation of friends and colleagues. Ah, a cup of nice, hot Peruvian...

What are "Cultural Buffers"?

The above parable derives from a simple "what if?": What if history had unfolded such that caffeine and cocaine switched places? Is it not true that, "Whether a drug is a vicious plague or an innocent beverage depends entirely on whose cartel got going first"? Surely we can believe this once we realize that cocaine can be enjoyed in the benign form of a mild tea whilst caffeine is quite a dangerous drug when had in purer forms. But the main point of the parable is to illustrate how "cultural buffers" might have come into place for cocaine, and might not have done so for caffeine, simply as a result of production and distribution cartels and their impact upon public usage.

Thus, Tom English is part of an imagined world where cocaine takes all the pleasant forms in everyday life that caffeine now does. It's in hot or cold drinks to restimulate the working day in midmorning or midafternoon. It enjoys the backing of colorful logos, familiar the world around. There are lots of different flavorings and brands to choose among. But usage is "accultured" and controlled in a number of ways– people often take their cocaine as part of a mealtime or breaktime ritual, and they are mindful that too much of this stimulant drug might get them overhyped or unable to sleep well, for which there are extremely mild forms ("decoke") available to give some of the pleasure without the deleterious effect. Meanwhile, caffeine users dwell in a very different world. Their drug is illegal, which means the users are fewer and more furtive– and younger and more prone to high risk behavior of all sorts. The powerful psychotropic impact of high-dose caffeine only adds to the outlaw character of "caff" scenes. And because caffeine trafficking is illegal, producers are motivated to concentrate and purify the active ingredient, if only because small quantities are easier to ship and smuggle.

So why has coffee flourished while coca– outside of a few regions of the Andes mountains– is everywhere suppressed? That question is best answered by asking another: "Why do stimulant drugs flourish at all?" The simple answer is that people need their "pick me ups", and the more active and energetic and "hardworking" a culture is, the more pick-me-ups are used. Thus, the quickening of European commerce and trade after 1492 provided both the reason for and source of new stimulant drugs. This quickening accelerated in the 18th and 19th centuries, as one by one European nations underwent industrialization, urbanization, and the clock-paced life of factories and offices.

Five non-European plants offered themselves to this grand commerce of stimulants: coffee (from East Africa and Arabia), tea (from South and East Asia), tobacco (from North America), chocolate (from Central America), and coca (from South America). The first four of these were the stimulus for developing huge plantation economies. Along with sugar and cotton, they were the reason for much of the movement of labor (including slave labor) and capital into the European colonies and dependencies. It can be argued that stimulant drugs plus sugar were the *principal* agents that shaped the New World from the Mason-Dixon line to the Rio de la Plata (from 39° North to 34° South). It can also be argued that two of these drugs, coffee and tea, were the principal agents shaping intellectual life in Western Europe during the Enlightenment, in the way that they brought together educated people in coffee houses and afternoon teas.

Coca was a latecomer to this glorious commerce, but it arrived strong in the last third of the 19th Century, in the form of stimulant elixirs such as early Coca-Cola and Vin Mariani. These drinks are brothers to the coca teas which had long been brewed in the Andes, and they are cousins to coffee or tea, beverages made more or less directly from the plant material. But the coca drinks had the misfortune to appear just as problems with the purer form (cocaine) were becoming apparent. The addictive problems of Sigmund Freud, Arthur Conan Doyle, and others were the cause of much scandal in the 1880s, resulting in the suppression of the milder forms of coca before they had secured a strong enough foothold in EuroAmerican consumption patterns. Thus was coca kicked out of the charmed circle of worldwide stimulant-drug cartels.

In the Parable, I implied that Irish and Irish-Americans were hardest hit by "caff", both as an exploited production workforce and as persecuted addicts. Black and Arab Americans occupy more privileged roles in my imaginary America. I firmly believe that history could easily have unfolded in this way– that European entrepreneurs, seeking a cheap labor force for the plantations for the psychoactive substances everyone craved, could have raided different shores; that particular substances presented in various strengths could have interacted with some ethnic cultures to yield high levels of abusive use; and that these same substances might have found effective "buffer" in other ethnic cultures. In the same way, if there had been much "speed" and no cocaine available in the American drug underworld, our country's stimulant problem might well have been overwhelmingly White.

Speed Exceptionalism

Cultural buffers just might work for cocaine, in one or more of the ways described above. There's far less hope for those buffers to work for that other great illicit stimulant drug, methamphetamine. "Speed", unlike all the other major licit and illicit substances– opiates, alcohol, caffeine, marijuana, sugar, tobacco, and cocaine– is far from any natural source. Speed must be manufactured by means of fairly sophisticated chemistry; there is no plant that provides a mild, organic form of the active ingredient. There are no long-enduring social patterns of use of mild, low-intensity forms of methamphetamine. The speed user has no equivalent of coca tea: the choice is either a very powerful "hit" or none at all.

Another way in which speed differs from its fellow substances is the extraordinary environmental damage done in the course of its manufacture. Most of the other substances have some impact– tobacco plants deplete soil fertility, sugar plantations smoke up the local atmosphere with their biannual burnings, illicit marijuana gardens trash up parts of public lands– but these are gentle on the land compared with the impact of methamphetamine "cooks". The byproducts of even a one-pound "cook" of speed are toxic indeed:

Methanol	Iodine
Red phosphorus	Hydriotic acid
Muriatic acid	Lye
Anhydrous ammonia	Acetone
Sulfuric acid	et cetera...

These byproducts are often simply left on site, or dumped into drains or ditches. The result is that structures and landscape become too dangerous for habitation and must be condemned. Moreover, the families and associates of the "cooker", particularly children, are often sickened by exposure to these toxic chemicals.

Yet another serious problem with speed is its extraordinary capacity for "ego enhancement". The user feels all-powerful and all good. The analogy to John Milton's Satan, as presented in *Paradise Lost*, is apt: the user becomes a beautiful angel, justified to challenge God and mankind. Simply put, he behaves like a selfish jerk– and often violently so. The aggressive, potentially violent aspects of speed use are even more characteristic of those who traffic in the drug as well as use it. Of course, the phenomenon of "ego enhancement" applies as well to cocaine use, but with a great difference: the enhancement lasts for a fraction of an hour rather than several hours.

A fourth way in which speed stands out as irredeemably problematic is its effect on disease transmission, above all HIV. Speed users feel invulnerable, and even those well-versed in HIV prevention information are inclined to put all caution aside during the powerful "high". Moreover, there is a proneness to "rough sex" and to prolonged stimulation without orgasm, i.e. a rubbing-raw which increases the odds of HIV transmission. There is also the confluence of promiscuous sexual encounters with potentially high-risk individuals, in a context where injection equipment may be used and shared.

For all these reasons, the optimal policy can be summed up as *speed exceptionalism*. Present efforts to eliminate methamphetamine production, trafficking, and usage should be continued, even intensified.

The Floodplain of Uppers

At the outset of Statehood, California faced the question: what to do with the great Sacramento River floodplain? Should we let it be, leaving the vast network of waterways, marshes, muddy plains, and wooded uplands as they had been for eons? Or should we build levees, forcing the Central Valley drainage into a few large channels, thus freeing huge acreage to be drained for farms and towns? Mostly, we chose to build the levees, which *usually* kept the waters where we wanted them...

In effect we faced the same choice with a pair of stimulant drugs derived from Latin American plants. Coming into California were sacks of coffee, for the European and American Forty-Niners; and also a few sacks of coca leaves, for the Chileans and Peruvians among the Argonauts. Such "uppers" were as inevitable as the Springtime floods: people *will have* their pick-me-up drugs.

We gave caffeine free rein to flood our State, making a vast plain of gently flowing brown liquid: a thousand muck-islands of Starbucks, a million rivulets of coffee and tea each morning. The floodplain is messy and fertile, enriched by the diurnal stimulation of ten million brains. Occurring amid this labyrinth of muck and mire are gentle benefits– a quickening of productivity and sociability– and also mild damages– jangled nerves, stained teeth, etc.

But we build levees, tall and strong, against cocaine. Ninety-eight percent of the floodplain of California humanity is *dry*, not even a cup of coca tea to wet the landscape. The other two percent is raging, rushing speed-energy, outlaw waters determined to run their course. A harsh apartheid prevails: the rivers are high, fierce, and isolated, and much anxious effort is expended to keep them in their place. And, as David Musto might put it (*The American Disease*, Oxford 3rd ed. 1999) every generation or so the levee bursts, much of the dry land gets soaked, and the destruction is great...

V.

The Parable of Three-Way War

Parable V.

Thirteen-Ball Pool: A Way to Experience Three-Way Conflict

Eight-Ball Pool is a splendid game for two players, or for four players in two teams of two. It's not so suitable for three players, one of whom must stand by impatiently waiting to play the winner between the other two. Luckily there is a new game, Thirteen-Ball Pool, that enables three to play together.

The table for Thirteen-Ball Pool is wider than that for Eight-Ball Pool. Instead of the 44" x 88", six-pocket design, we have a 66" x 88", eight-pocket playing area arranged like this:

Thirteen-Ball requires 25 balls, of three different coloring patterns. Much as in Eight-Ball, the balls numbered 1

through 8 are "solids", while 9 through 12 and 14 through 17 are "stripes". Those numbered 18 through 25, the "checks", are colored in a checkerboard fashion. The seven traditional colors are used, with chartreuse employed for the eighth ball of each pattern:

#1, 9, and 18 are yellow
#5, 14, and 22 are orange
#3, 11, and 20 are red
#7, 16, and 24 are plum
#4, 12, and 21 are purple
#2, 10, and 19 are blue
#6, 15, and 23 are green
#8, 17, and 25 are chartreuse

Ball #13 is solid black. The game is won by the first player to sink all eight balls of his pattern, and thereafter to sink the 13-ball.

The initial setup requires a diagonal rather than a triangular rack. The balls are racked in this arrangement:

```
    A
   B B
  C C C
 B A A B
A C X C A
 B A A B
  C C C
   B B
    A
```

A = solids   C = checks
B = stripes   X = 13-ball

The three players draw lots to determine the order of play. The color pattern of the first ball sunk by each player then decides which set he tries to clear: solids, stripes, or checks.

Thirteen-Ball Pool enjoys several novel features:

- The number 13, in all its sinister majesty, holds the fulcrum of the game. That's a great improvement; poor little Eight has never been up to the job, as it's just too everyday and easygoing a number.

- The eight-pocket table permits a challenging version not possible in Eight-Ball, namely one where each player must sink each of the eight balls of his set into a different pocket.

- In bars and pool halls, each game of Eight-Ball typically costs 75¢. It's only fair that a game of Thirteen-Ball costs twice as much, because it typically lasts longer and the table occupies more of the establishment's space.

- But the most valuable facet of Thirteen-Ball Pool is the manifestation of the dynamic of three-way conflict. Three players can in a single game match skills with one another, an exercise that would necessitate three separate Eight-Ball games. The dynamic is immediate and continual: whenever one player takes time to plan and execute his shot, the other two are free to draw together for a few moments of quiet disparagement or conspiring. Such a pairing is soon broken, for one of them must take his turn to shoot, giving the odd-man-out his own opportunity for quiet plotting with the other member of the pair. And then it will be the third player's turn to shoot, and a chance for the third conspiring twosome to form. Thus it goes, round after round, making each game a rich panoply of shifting alliances, betrayals, and reconciliations, especially as two losing players work together to prevent the leading player from clinching victory.

An evening of Thirteen-Ball among three friends will typically be characterized by cascading episodes of resentful isolation, unexpected support, graceful teamwork, subtle double-dealing, sudden entrapment, and perhaps an exasperated free-for-all. The three will end their evening exhausted but matured. They will have come to a deeper understanding of the three-way conflicts that have enriched human history– Serbs versus Croats versus Muslims, paper versus scissors versus rock, Carreras versus Domingo versus Pavarotti, and so forth.

A General Theory of Drug Abuse Policy

Players of Thirteen-Ball Pool will gain a keen appreciation of the arena of drug abuse policy where, after all, not two but three philosophies contend: "The User as Needful Human Being" versus "The User as Willful Criminal" versus "The User as Taxpaying Citizen". These drug-policy philosophies are just one expression of the traditional tripartite conflicts in American political life– Left versus Hard Right versus Libertarian Right– which may enjoy especially vivid expression in the near future.

The three philosophies– grossly simplified– can be summarized thus:

The **Social Welfare Strategy** derives from the belief that people abuse drugs because of deprivation. People want an escape from lives empty of job opportunities, or meaningful education, or decent housing, or proper healthcare, or rewarding personal relationships. Substance use can alleviate this emptiness for a time, but use often leads to abuse, and underprivileged people have few resources to overcome that abuse. But just remove the deprivations, say the Social Welfare strategists, and most of the reason to abuse drugs and alcohol will disappear. Of course, this strategy is expensive: it means creating a minimum standard of living and expanded opportunities for education and employment. That, in turn, means higher taxes on "those who can afford it".

The **War on Drugs Strategy** views America as a decent, law-abiding, sober majority in conflict with a recalcitrant, rebellious drug-abusing minority. If people would just obey the law, everything would be OK. But force is required to encourage obedience: harsher and harsher penalties must be levied on drug traffickers, and more and more firepower brought against the producers, until the evil is finally eliminated. The deviant drug abuser or trafficker must be punished not only to "correct" his behavior but to salve the morale of the law-abiding majority.

Adherents of the **Legalize/Regulate/Tax Strategy** view substance use as a private matter. They are willing to let people use alcohol, tobacco, heroin, cocaine, or whatever, providing there isn't a clear intrusion on the welfare of others. If they get addicted, tough luck– they made a free choice and must take responsibility for the consequences. Under this strategy, all psychoactive substances are legal; but there are regulations to assure minimum standards of purity and quality, to prevent sales to minors, and to favor milder over stronger forms of each drug (e.g., beer over gin, coca tea over crack, laudanum over heroin). Each drug is taxed to cover the costs of regulation and of the "downstream" healthcare costs, and also to pay for public education campaigns to discourage people (especially adolescents) from using in the first place. The regulating and taxing, in effect, is a payoff to the non-using public to gain their consent.

It's instructive to quote some favorite buzzwords and phrases for each strategy. For the Social Welfare advocates, "justice", "equality", "redistribution of wealth", "client services", "meaningful work", "affirmative action", "benefits", and "they're depraved because they're deprived" all are valued concepts. For the War on Drugs people, "crush", "war", "get tough", "sick and tired", "eliminate", "orderly society", and "beat some sense into them" stir the blood. And with the Legalize/Tax/Regulate faction, "liberty", "privacy", "give them what they want", "get the government out of our private lives", and "at their own risk" are music to the ears.

My hypothesis is that the advocates of these strategies fight a three-way struggle in which, in America, no one of them is ever strong enough to overcome the other two. Whereas there can be at-least-temporary winners in a two-way struggle, a three-way conflict may be perpetually stalemated if (as I believe is the case) the three are fairly evenly matched. Whenever one strategy begins to gain the upper hand, the other two mercilessly badger it from two sides to weaken it. So: *of course* Social Welfare could raise everyone out of poverty, as it has in Sweden, but somehow in the America of the past generation we lost the will to keep funding all of the splendid programs of the War on Poverty and to run them effectively. *Of course* the War on Drugs could prevail, given the unlimited police power of the Gestapo or the K.G.B.; but in present-day America, social welfare advocates tirelessly defend the rights of the accused, and the humdrum realities of policing the inner cities leads to a kind of *de facto* legalization: the War becomes a velvet fist in an iron glove. And *of course* Legalize/Regulate/Tax could transform a nasty problem into a relatively benign one, as it has in the Netherlands, but somehow in the America of the 1970s when we started that way with marijuana, we only went halfway with Legalize and never secured the Regulate and Tax payoffs.

From the user's point of view, society is persistently giving a muddled triple message: "You're a troubled human being in need of help"– "You're a drug fiend who ought to be in prison"– "You're a citizen who should be left to mind his own business". As a result the moral authority of society is weak, leaving the user's relationship to The Drug as the central organizing principle and source of meaningfulness in life.

Three-Way Conflict and Perpetual Stalemate

I postulate that there are two overriding realities about American politics that will constrain policymaking in the substance abuse arena throughout the foreseeable future:

- The anti-tax climate is so strong that no major new initiatives for public expenditure can be funded. Federal deficits (the excess of expenditures over income) are putting great pressure on "discretionary" spending. The best that advocates in any arena can expect is an incremental increase.

- Policymakers, Democrat and Republican, have so stridently declared themselves against the legalization of drugs that no reversal can be expected for many years.

Now, any truly effective manifestation of the Social Welfare or the War on Drugs Strategies would require a massive infusion of tax moneys for anti-poverty programs or for policing of inner cities, borders, and suchlike. But this is not the era of Lyndon Johnson; those massive infusions aren't going to happen, because taxpayers won't permit it. Therefore, both the Social Welfare and the War on Drugs Strategies will remain in their present emasculated state. But there is similarly no hope on the horizon for effective implementation of the Legalize/Regulate/Tax Strategy, because no major politician would dare to be the first to advocate it.

My second hypothesis, then, is that there is a fourth drug policy strategy to which America will, for the above reasons, default: the **Laissez-Faire Strategy**. Adherents to this Strategy believe that substance abuse problems are basically cyclical, and will wax and wane on their own account regardless of our muddled attempts at intervention. Therefore, the essential tactic in each situation is to keep calm and avoid wasting energy. The goal is to maneuver to avoid any new laws, taxes, or policies, but instead perpetuate existing mechanisms for minimizing the harm that drug use does. The inclination is always toward the passive, with occasional forays to delay, dilute, negate, or otherwise frustrate the activist initiatives of the Social Welfare, War on Drugs, or Legalize/Regulate/Tax Strategies.

From this hypothesis we may derive a simple prediction: twenty years hence the drug abuse situation in America will be essentially the same as it is now. The familiar gamut of treatment modalities will serve clients and claim successes. There will be lip service to some sort of War on Drugs, with the occasional major media-splashed bust of a drug cartel from Country X and the seizure of many kilos of drug Y. And most illicit drugs will be cheap and easily available, and people will abuse them in their millions.

So, I predict that in the year 2027:

- There will be, as now, a million or so Americans using heroin.
- They will pay, as now, a dollar or so for each milligram of heroin.
- Most of them will use the needle and be at risk for parenteral infection, specifically HIV and HCV.
- Marijuana use will be about as widespread as it is now (or, indeed, as it has been for the past 30 years).

But what Strategy will prevail in 2027, in response to these facts-on-the-ground? Will the three primary

Strategies continue to cancel out one another, and allow Laissez-Faire to prevail by default?

For a while in the late 1990s and early 2000s the War on Drugs approach appeared on the verge of triumph. That Strategy was helped by Republican dominance of much of the Federal and States' executive and legislative branches, and by public acceptance of draconian penalties for drug trafficking. The numbers of people incaracerated on drug charges reflect these stringent policies. Between 1983 and 1998, the annual rate of incarceration to state and federal prisons rose from just over 11,000 to 170,000– a 16-fold increase. The increase in those 15 years was far greater for Hispanics (18-fold) and Blacks (26-fold) than for Whites (seven-fold). By 1998, nearly one in four persons in state and local prisons– and nearly three in five in federal prisons– was there for violating a specific drug law.

While these dramatic increases in the prison population were occurring, the public at large was becoming *less* anxious about drug use. According to the Gallup Poll, the proportions of respondents describing drug use as "the single most important problem facing our country" fell steadily over a fifteen-year period:

1989	17%
1994	9%
1999	5%
2004	1%

The severity of cuts in public spending puts pressure on both the War on Drugs and Social Welfare Strategies, as each, for obvious reasons, are huge consumers of public funds. It seems that the public feels each has had a good trial, and each is just too expensive, and we've got better things to do with our scarce tax dollars, therefore... but what about Legalize/Tax/Regulate? Will Americans abandon their long-enduring Puritanism and embrace this Strategy? Polls cast doubt on this possibility– for example Pew Research Center data on what people in 2001 believed was "the most effective actions the government could take to control the use of drugs":

30% said "arrest drug users in the country"
36% said "provide drug treatment programs for drug users"

At about this same time, a National Opinion Research Center survey found that 34% of American adults believed that marijuana should be made legal.

The foregoing three percentages reflect the current stalemate of drug use policy: three distinct points of view each command a substantial minority but are well short of a majority.

I don't believe either the Social Welfare or the War on Drugs Strategy has much chance in the next 20 years, for the simple reason that they're both very expensive and government spending is simply too constrained by tax cuts and Social Security/Medicare costs. Of course the "one last laughing push to bring down the preposterous edifice of the Drug War" (see Introduction) could happen at any time, ushering in the triumph of the Legalize/Tax/Regulate Strategy. But I see this as likelier in the more distant future.

So I propose one more prediction for the America of 2027:

- The Laissez-Faire Strategy will continue to dominate policymaking, and we will continue to muddle through confusedly just as we have for the past 30 years.

* * * * * * *

The paradigm of "three-way war" is prominent in the social and political life of our country. The commonest, but not the only, form taken is that of hard right versus libertarian versus social-welfare left. In many cases the libertarian point of view– basically, "don't help, don't hassle, don't burden the rest of us with costs"– is strong enough to ensure an enduring three-way conflict. Such enduring conflicts are the case now in such areas as immigration policy, attitudes toward gays, and the regulation of prostitution. The three-way war paradigm goes far to explaining why policy conflicts persist, decade after decade, without resolution.

The second half of this book will expand on the theme of three-way war, with the basic contention that the tripartite stalemate will persist for another 10 or 20 years, but that sheer exhaustion will lead to the eventual triumph of a Legalize/Tax/Regulate policy framework. But first, an interlude to elucidate more fully what this "libertarian" policy consists of.

INTERLUDE

"There never was a good war, nor a bad peace"

At time of changes in government we have a chance to rethink our "War on Drugs". I regard that war as a catastrophic failure, and I am reminded that there is an alternative peace strategy, summarized thus:

> "Legalize drugs. Then tax them so that government gets most of the profits. Use the tax revenue to regulate the drug market and to run campaigns to discourage use. In other words, just as for tobacco."

Here are "meditations" and "commentaries" on each part of the Peace strategy:

(1) "Legalize Drugs"

Meditation. Imagine an America with a fraction of the current numbers of young people in prison, on parole, or on probation. Imagine inner cities where the main cause of alienation from the police has vanished. Visualize headlines on the closing down of prisons, in response to ever-declining inmate numbers.

Commentary. Many thousands of Americans are in prison solely for drug possession. Hundreds of thousands more were convicted for trafficking, or for property crimes related to supporting drug usage. Blacks are far more often criminalized than Whites: more than twice as many are serving sentences for drug offenses (133,100 versus 64,800 in 2005), though White Americans outnumber Blacks by six to one and have comparable usage rates of illegal drugs. Meanwhile, each of the four major illegal drugs has a legal cousin (heroin = alcohol, cocaine = caffeine, speed = tobacco, marijuana = sugar) which serves the same basic human needs of pain relief, "attitude adjustment", "pick me up", sheer pleasure, etc. The pairs differ mostly because of price, strength, and legality, and it is easy to conceive a world where the roles are switched.

We advocates of legalization agree with Drug War supporters that *drug use is a serious problem.* The difference is that we see no role for law enforcement in resolving this problem; it is a job for health professionals and self-help groups. Or, as Brendan Behan might have put it, "There is no manifestation of addictive disease that cannot be made worse by the involvement of the police".

Meditation. Now recall the one day in your life during which you suffered most from chronic coughing. Visualize taking a cough syrup that gave you prompt, soothing relief.

Commentary. The War on Drugs hurts our society not only because it criminalizes *some* people, but also because it impedes the rest of us from enjoying the real benefits of those substances. Relief from chronic coughing was a very real benefit for me. At age seven I contracted whooping cough, and experienced coughing spells of such violence that I nearly broke my ribs, and was hard put to catch my breath. The syrup which gave prompt relief was terpin hydrate of codeine. The three-minute transition from spasms and terror, to blessed relief, was as profound as any I have experienced in my life. But, in 2007, it is much more difficult for such suffering to be thus relieved. The illegality of opiates makes their benefits almost unobtainable for the majority of us who are at no risk for abuse.

(2) "...tax them..."

Meditation. Visualize the suitcases full of cash that change hands in major drug deals. Picture the billionaire wealth of the greatest drug barons, such as the Escobars. Now visualize those suitcases of cash used to purchase space and amenities for Twelve Step groups. Imagine the wealth of the Escobars creating places like Delancey Street and Walden House– *hundreds* of them.

Commentary. A sound approach to industrial pollution is to tax each factory enough to pay the costs of cleaning up the mess it causes. This has the double benefit of encouraging factories to be less polluting, and assuaging public anger because the factory, not the public, now pays the cleanup costs. In just such a way, our society should tax substances in proportion to their "downstream" costs. Substances whose use results in few bad consequences, such as marijuana and coffee, would be taxed lightly; substances with nastier consequences, such as alcohol and opiates, would be taxed more heavily. Tobacco, the deadliest of all, would be taxed most of all– 10 dollars a pack would be about right. The tax revenues would go partly to treat diseases such as emphysema and abscesses, and partly to fund programs to support abstinence.

Of course, the more profitable an enterprise, the more tax revenue can fairly be derived from it. Legalized drugs should be marketed through the rich creativity of entrepreneurs, not the dull hand of the State: thus a few cents worth of coca leaves can become a $3 cup of coca tea in a pleasant bistro, just as a few cents worth of coffee beans become a $3 cup of latte in a Starbucks.

(3) "...regulate the drug market..."

Meditation. Visualize a society where opiates, cocaine, and marijuana are as legal as alcohol and tobacco– but also as tightly regulated. The formerly illegal drugs are now bought at stores and even at "bars", but the entrepreneurs who operate these outlets are licensed and carefully monitored. Their business is profitable, but they fear losing their license if they sell to anyone under 21, or if they cheat on taxes. Moreover, the tax and regulatory structures heavily favor the milder forms of the drugs: low-THC marijuana, opiates as dilute laudanum syrup, cocaine as coca tea. There are more users, but these larger numbers create new norms of controlled usage: intoxication is frowned upon, "we are here to enjoy ourselves, not to get crazy".

Commentary. This is the great payoff for HIV and HCV prevention. The primary goal of such prevention among drug users is to reduce the incidence of sharing injection equipment. A legal, regulated market for opiates and stimulants achieves that goal in four ways:

- The tax and regulatory structures can favor milder forms of the drug. Intoxication– if desired– would be achieved by lots of liquid, drunk, rather than a little powder, injected.

- Open and legal usage means that strictures– formal and informal– against dangerous needle use are more readily applied.

- With the psychoactive substance readily available, users will rarely be in a rush; they have the time to ingest their chosen substance with care.

• Even if people choose to shoot up, injection and disinfection equipment– themselves now legal– could be readily available.

Legalization is very helpful in ending the HIV epidemic among users of opiates and stimulants. But legalization is, I believe, the *only* way to end the hepatitis C epidemic among such users. Our present prevention strategies– needle exchange, bleach distribution, and outreach education– are *hopelessly inadequate* in the face of a virus which is so much less forgiving of "slips" than is HIV. The only real hope is a society-wide change in the way opiates and stimulants are used, such that, even for those craving a powerful "kick", routes other than intravenous are preferred.

(4) "...run campaigns to discourage use..."

Meditation. Reflect on what has happened to tobacco use in California in the last 40 years. Public smoking disappeared, first from elevators, then from buses and airplanes, then from restaurants and offices, and finally from bars. A hefty tobacco tax was enacted, and the revenue was used to create clever campaigns to discourage smoking. Forty years ago, 40% of adult men smoked; now, barely 15% do. All without sending a single person to prison for using tobacco, or burning a single tobacco field.

Commentary. Just as campaigns against tobacco use succeeded without forbidding [adult] usage, campaigns against use of opiates, cocaine, and marijuana can succeed in a context of legal [adult] access. A well-designed public information campaign can make the bad aspects of a drug clear *and credible.* We merely need to tell the truth, vividly. We should say, in essence, "Most any drug is safe, and even beneficial, if used moderately and in mild forms; but beware the signs of habitual or addictive use, and beware intoxication".

Jon Gettman nicely summarizes these four components in regard to pot (*Marijuana Production in the United States, 2006*): "Like all profitable agricultural crops marijuana adds resources and value to the economy...The focus for public policy should be how to effectively control this market through regulation and taxation in order to achieve immediate and realistic goals, such as reducing teenage access." Gettman estimates that 22,000,000 pounds of domestic marijuana were harvested in 2006, with a value of $35.8 billion. Even "light" taxation of this crop, if legalized, would have produced billions in revenue to our commonwealth.

* * * * * * * *

In summary, there are three great reasons why even a flawed Peace is preferable to the War on Drugs. (1) We can't afford to criminalize and alienate millions of people in a racially biased way. (2) We don't deserve to have criminal gangs getting rich on substance-use revenue which rightly belongs to honest entrepreneurs and the tax-paying public. (3) Our hypocrisy around legal and illegal substances is an existential sickness that corrupts American culture.

Outlining a peace policy is the easy part. Far tougher is the question, how do we get from here to there? How do we end the War and create a new world of legalize, tax, regulate, discourage?

CINCINNATUS AT HIS FARM

PONDERING THE PLEA OF THE CITY TO RETURN TO THE WAR ON DRUGS

Interlude

In 1985 I produced the first wine from my vineyard at Green Valley Ranch in the Napa Valley. I thereby exemplified, "if you can't lick 'em, join 'em": I joined the multitudes of winemakers, brewers, barmen, B-girls, tobacconists, coffeeshop owners, dealers, sommeliers, pot farmers, distillers, and other involved in the merry everyday business of making and selling psychoactive substances, legal and illegal. Often I would sit with my dogs across the lake from my vineyard, reflecting on all the people I'd never meet who would drink my wine and say, "Hey, this stuff is really *good!*" And I would think about the War on *some* of these substances, and how I was being called back to it, and I'd wonder, "Should I go back? And if so, *which side should I fight on*?"

VI.

The Parable of Evaporation

Parable VI.

Evaporation

On occasion, a great and mighty social force will simply "evaporate" from the stage of history without ever being decisively confronted or defeated. The supreme example is Napoleon's Grand Army. This force of 600,000 men, led by the military genius who had conquered Europe, fought its way successfully to Moscow in the summer of 1812. It lingered there through September, hoping in vain that Czar Alexander would sue for peace. Leo Tolstoy, in *War and Peace*, describes what happened next:

> After the French victory at Borodino there was no general engagement nor any that were at all serious, yet the French army ceased to exist...
>
> There was no forage for the horses or the cattle...the peasants of the district burned their hay rather than let the French have it...
>
> The members of what had once been an army– Napoleon himself and all his soldiers– fled without knowing whither, each concerned only to make his escape as quickly as possible from this position, of the hopelessness of which they were all more or less vaguely conscious...they all went without knowing whither or why they were going...each was thinking only of himself and of how to get away quickly and save himself.

The destruction of the Grand Army was akin to evaporation: a gradual, little-by-little process by which a huge force vanished without any sudden traumas. Tolstoy likened it to "melting away at the uniform rate of a mathematical progression." I believe a similar thing is happening in San Francisco to a social force that, while anything but grand, has nonetheless powerfully affected life in this city for decades: burglary. The class of people who commit burglaries is evaporating away, little by little, almost without anyone noticing it. Here is the evidence:

Reported Burglaries, San Francisco, 1976-2000

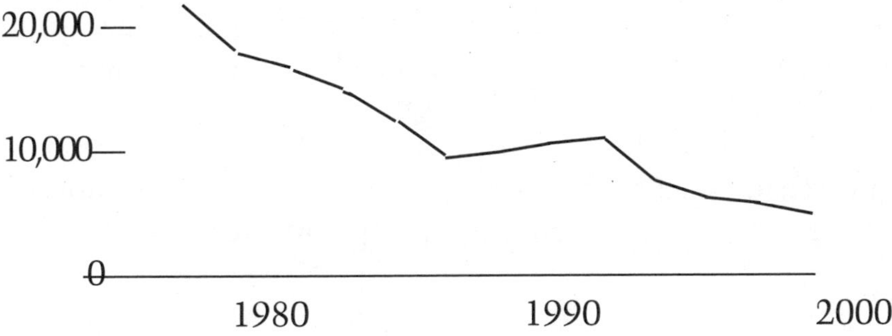

The rate of reported burglaries has fallen by *more than three-quarters* since 1976. Lest we think this unprecedented decline is an artifact of decreased reporting, or merely part of a statewide trend, here are burglary data for Vallejo, a small city 30 miles northeast of San Francisco:

Reported Burglaries, Vallejo, 1976-1998

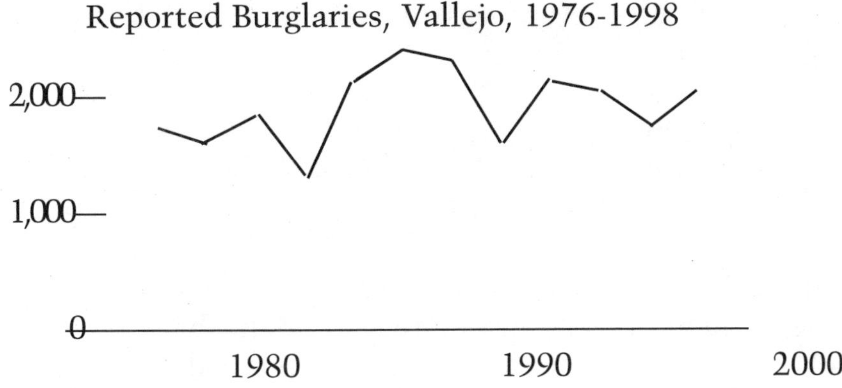

I hypothesize that certain conditions have prevailed in San Francisco to cause rapid "evaporation" of the burglar class in the past two decades. I also hypothesize that this evaporation will continue, and that two other classes of people– heroin users and speed users– will also be evaporating.

In 1812, Napoleon's army disappeared not because it was overpowered by the Russian army, but for economic reasons: there was not enough food, not enough forage, not enough shelter, not enough winter clothing. These days, people heavily into the drug scenes evaporate away from San Francisco not because of police vigilance, but for economic reasons. The main reason is that they are "downwardly mobile", experiencing disruptions such as

- job loss
- jail terms
- family instability
- evictions
- "hit the road, Jack!", i.e. female householders no longer permitting drug-using boyfriends to shack up with them

in a city where there is vastly expanded gentrification of neighborhoods, leading to

- rising property values and rents
- increased neighborhood cohesion and "vigilance"
- fewer vacant lots or buildings

Evaporation happens to burglars, speed users, and heroin users little by little. For one reason or another, they can't go back to live where they used to, and they can't get it together to find a new place to live in the incredibly competitive housing environment of San Francisco. So they leave, one by one, unnoticed, perhaps to "precipitate" nearby in Vallejo or Fremont or Daly City. The result is that San Francisco's burglary rate has plummeted, and so will its prevalence of speed users and heroin users. This phenomenon is well under way in a few other "gentrifying" cities, most notably San Jose, Manhattan, and Boston.

Commentary

In the face of this "evaporation", will the population of injection drug users in San Francisco gradually decline to zero? Or will pockets of users endure in the face of the economic factors cited above? I believe three classes of IDUs will hang on, at least for some years:

• **Bourgeois Bohemians.** "Bobos" are eloquently described in David Brooks' book, *Bobos in Paradise.* "Bobos" are able to thrive in the middle-class world of high-paying jobs, family responsibilities, homeownership, etc., while simultaneously enjoying a freewheeling, casual lifestyle. That lifestyle can include use of marijuana, Ecstasy, psychedelics, perhaps even injected heroin or speed. Such "controlled" use of injected drugs is nearly invisible, because the key indicators (overdose deaths, emergency-room visits, publicly-funded treatment, arrests) rarely detect it.

• **Downwardly-Mobile Middle Class**. I've noticed that about one-third of the clients seen at Haight-Ashbury Free Clinic Detox for primary heroin problems report that they've had at least some college education. Such individuals can be described as having been on a path to middle-class status– though the majority of them were jobless by the time they entered treatment there. They are downwardly mobile: they enter adulthood with considerable assets but gradually lose them. However, it takes years for hard drug use to degrade those assets to the point where the user can no longer keep it together to stay in San Francisco.

• **The Homeless**. By simply living on the street, one avoids having to cope with the high cost of living in this city. A large number of people (estimates run as high as 14,000) are surviving in this way, and a substantial minority of them use injectable drugs at least occasionally. They are particularly at risk for HIV and HCV infection because of their living conditions. However, few of them can manage steady heroin or speed habits: injectable drugs are expensive and cash is short, and the option of cheap vodka ($4 per pint) is always available.

I predict that these three groups will dominate the IDU population by 2010, having supplanted the working-class users who had predominated among IDUs here for the past 30 years. Around that year, I predict, the IDU population will level off at about half of the current level of 15,000. These survivors will be about equally divided among the three groups mentioned above, with the working-class user group almost completely "evaporated".

* * * * * * *

Evaporation can be seen as another aspect of the "Wal-Martization of America". Wal-Mart is all about *cheap*– wonderfully cheap goods of all sorts, but also cheap labor. Even fulltime Wal-Mart employees have a median annual income of barely $19,000. The corporation is also notoriously stingy about healthcare coverage for its workers. The result is that Wal-Marts and poor people find one another, in parts of America well away from rich suburbs and prospering inner cities. It is to these areas that "evaporated" substance abusers will, little by little, "precipitate". We should expect this country's speed scene to flourish in such areas, and not in Manhattan or San Francisco or San Diego.

Substance abuse is not the only reason for disruption of

lives and consequent forced migration. A more important reason is the disappearance of so many traditional working-class jobs. There are fewer things for a poorly-educated American to do to earn good money. Manual labor of all sorts can be "outsourced" to eager low-wage workers in Asia and Latin America, And low-wage workers with a command of English– in India or Barbados, for example– can do much of the work heretofore done by Americans at computer terminals or telephone exchanges. Even professional jobs are not safe from outsourcing; one thinks of surgery patients heading to Thailand or architectural projects farmed out to Taiwan.

Likewise, the role of welfare recipient lost 4.7 million "slots" after the 1996 Welfare Reform law. Where are these Americans to live? As with substance abusers, any disruption– divorce, eviction, the loss of a job– can put them "on the road". In essence this is downward mobility– moving to a less desirable part of the country and losing supportive connections to family and friends.

At the same time, great numbers of well-educated citizens are also migrating in an upwardly mobile direction. Richard Florida analyzed the relative attractiveness of American urban areas to "knowledge workers" (*The Rise of the Creative Class: And how it's Transforming Work, Leisure, Community and Everyday Life*, Basic Books, 2002). The basic trend is clear: highly-educated Americans prefer places like New York, Boston, and the San Francisco Bay Area over "heartland" places such as Amarillo, Birmingham, and Omaha.

These two migrations are akin to the gradual separation of oil and water from a once well-shaken bottle of salad dressing. Increasingly, the rich and poor live separated from one another. This will inevitably lead to a redistribution of America's "geography of drug usage."

There is a subtle form of evaporation, not about migration but about demography. In their controversial book (*Freakonomics: A Rogue Economist Explores the Hidden Side of Everything*, 2005) Steven Levitt and Stephen Dubner advance the notion that America's crime rate dropped in the 1990s because abortion was made legal in 1973. Roe versus Wade enabled far more poor women to abort unwanted children, which cut the numbers of children raised in dysfunctional households, which in turn cut the number of youths (especially boys) inclined to delinquency in the 1990s. What goes for crime may also go for substance abuse: a reduction in the number of low socioeconomic status delinquents could account for the decline of heroin and cocaine use in the 1995-2005 era.

VII.

The Parable of the Sick Liver

Parable VII.

The Secret Sharer

"See, it's this way, doc," Joe declared, "I shot heroin for a couple of years back in '85-'86. The first five or six times I shared works with the guys I was running with in the projects. But then I heard about AIDS and how bad it was getting for the junkies, so I got real paranoid real fast. The whole rest of the time I used, I was real careful to have my own works, or when I couldn't, to bleach the needle real good."

"So then– you knew all about HIV disease 20 years ago, and you knew how to protect yourself?" inquired Dr. Kazan, as he flipped through Joe's thin medical file.

"You bet I did! And I also used condoms whenever I screwed around with women other than my honey. She and me have been together ever since I got clean at the beginning of '87."

"So you're pretty sure you don't have HIV?"

"I was real confident about that until just last year, when I started feeling those low energy episodes I told you about," replied Joe. "I knew that the only risk I had was those five or six sharing times, and the research guy at the clinic said that I probably got away OK, 'cause each sharing has only about a 1% risk. And anyway I was fine for all those years, so I never took the AIDS test until here just last week."

"Then this is the first time you've ever heard your HIV status?" said the doctor, as he turned to Joe's test results.

"Yup. And I'm really, really anxious right now," replied Joe, "I'd hate to think that I got infected after all that time of being so careful. What's the result, doc, do I have that HIV? Is my blood sick?"

"No, Joe, your blood is fine, your HIV test came back negative..."

"*Awwwright!*" he yelled, pumping the air with his fist. "I'm a clean guy! I'm gonna call the wife right away..."

"But your liver is sick-- your lipids are way up, and I'm sorry to say, you tested positive for hepatitis C."

Hepatitis C: The Great Time Bomb

Antibody tests for hepatitis C have only been available since 1989, and it is only in the last several years that the disease has gotten the widespread attention it merits. The importance of the hepatitis C virus (HCV) in our lives can be summed up in three sentences:

- About 3,900,000 Americans are now infected with HCV and at least 30,000 more get infected each year.

- Of those infected, at least 80% will be chronic "carriers", capable of infecting others; and about 17% will develop cirrhosis.

- Of those infected, about 5% will die as a direct result of liver disease, principally cirrhosis or liver cancer.

HCV is a "time bomb" in that progression to cirrhosis typically takes 20 years. Moreover, most HCV+ people are unaware of their infection and may continue to engage in practices (especially alcohol and drug use) which accelerate disease progress and/or get other people infected.

It would seem, then, that the current level of HCV infection will directly result in the death of 195,000 Americans (5% of 3,900,000) unless there are major improvements in treatment. That number of deaths is greater than that of all but two of America's wars– and almost on a scale with the mortality of the Civil War (527,000), World War II (405,000), or AIDS (570,000 by 2006). Moreover, *liver disease is expensive*, which means we all will pay a bit more through our health plans and Medicare taxes to cover costs of dialyses, liver transplants, and other pricey interventions occasioned by people's HCV disease.

Clearly, hepatitis C is poised to be one of the major diseases killing Americans early in the new century. What does this mean for our country's injection drug users?

Comparing Two Epidemics

HCV infection occurs mostly because of blood-to-blood contacts via shared hypodermic equipment, tattoo needles, razors, and suchlike. Injection drug users (IDUs) are the #1 risk group for HCV, and comprise about half of all infected Americans. HCV transmits more readily than HIV through shared "rigs", as evidenced by the fact that about 70% of all American IDUs are HCV+, while only about 18% are HIV+. IDU infection rates in San Francisco– a city which has benefited from many years of bleach distribution, needle exchange, and other energetic prevention measures– are roughly 55% for HCV and 10% for HIV.

The good news is that HCV is transmitted *less* readily than HIV through sexual intercourse, or from mother to child. The evidence for this is that only about 5% of steady heterosexual partners of HCV+ persons are themselves infected, while a similarly small percentage of babies of HCV+ mothers are infected. People with multiple sexual partners, and people who engage in receptive anal intercourse are at somewhat higher risk. This means that gay men are at significant risk for HCV; however, I believe that more gay Americans have been infected by parenteral practices (heavy "speed" use in particular) than by sexual activities.

Gay men used to comprise the largest group of Americans infected with HIV each year, but since the early 1990s IDUs are the #1 HIV risk group, as they've always been for

HCV. I have done very rough estimates of how HCV and HIV are impacting IDUs. (For purposes of this essay, I define "IDU" as any person, gay or straight, who has injected drugs more than three times in the past 20 years.)

Prevalence

1,750,000 American IDUs are HCV+ (that's about 70% of 2,500,000 American IDUs; and it's about 45% of the 3,900,000 HCV+ Americans)

450,000 American IDUs are HIV+

Incidence

80,000 American IDUs are infected with HCV each year
20,000 American IDUs are infected with HIV each year

The prevalence of HCV among IDUs is approximately four times that for HIV. Likewise, the annual incidence of new HCV infections is roughly four times that for HIV. Because HIV is about eight times as lethal as HCV– some 40% of HIV-infected Americans have died of AIDS, and we expect about 5% of HCV-infected people to die of liver disease– we can make the rough approximation that hepatitis C will ultimately kill half as many people as has HIV. The critical difference is that *the future belongs to HCV*. In 1994 about 15,000 IDUs died of AIDS. In 2007, thanks mostly to combination therapies, only about 7,000 will die– and there is reason to hope the death rate will continue to decline. Meanwhile, IDU deaths consequent to HCV are rising steadily and– barring treatment improvements– will reach an annual rate in the 4,000-5,000 range within the next decade, and remain there for many years thereafter.

The Coming Transition

The epidemiology of HCV is still in very poor focus, so it must be borne in mind that the above numbers are mere approximations; they could easily be wrong by 20%. But they are good for a rough picture, in which the main feature is that *HCV is well placed to replace HIV as the #1 disease threat to IDUs.*

I visualize a transition toward a new world of "HCV experts" not unlike the present world of "AIDS experts", whose main enterprise will be to create a system of care for the millions of Americans facing liver disease. Here are three predictions about what that new world will be like:

- HCV prevention among IDUs will be tougher because we'll be asking them to act now to prevent potential sickness that's not merely 10 years away, as with AIDS, but 20 or 30 years. That's a tough sell for people whose concerns are so much focused on the here and now. Moreover, a friendship network of IDUs may encompass a 10-year span of "user careers" but not a 20- or 30-year span, which means the newest users are likely to know (and be influenced by) someone dealing with AIDS, but they won't know anyone yet "old" enough to have developed liver disease.

- HCV prevention among IDUs will also be tougher because they'll need to achieve "100% safe parenteral practices" more nearly. With HIV, there's perhaps a one-in-150 chance of becoming infected if you use a rig after someone who's HIV+, and only 15% of users are HIV+. But with HCV, it's more like a one-in-10 chance of infection in a world where 55% of users are HCV+. Thus, the world of HCV is much less forgiving of occasional "slips" than the world of HIV.

• The politics will be less crazy, mainly because most HCV is transmitted by sharing blood-tainted equipment rather than by sexual intercourse. In the new world of the "Standard Model of HCV Care", there won't so much hindrance from homophobic or puritan policymakers, and there won't be a squeamish reluctance to voice the words, "cirrhosis" or "liver failure". On the other side, an aggressive public health campaign aimed at reducing HCV contagion won't arouse so much opposition from advocates anxious to protect the civil rights of sexual minorities.

Can HCV Be Prevented Among Injection Drug Users?

Two Epidemics Compared

HCV, like HIV, spreads among IDUs by means of sharing contaminated injection equipment. Unlike HIV infection, *most* HCV infection in the U.S. is among current and former IDUs. Is there hope that a campaign to prevent the spread of HCV will enjoy the same success as that against HIV? The short answer seems to be, "No, not without a much more diligent and comprehensive public health campaign". Following are three critical differences between HIV and HCV which serve to toughen the prevention challenge for the latter.

Problem One: This Virus Spreads *Fast*

As regards prevention, the key difference between the two viruses is that HCV is *much more unforgiving of slips.* There are two reasons for this: the probability of HCV transmission from a single risky slip is much higher, and the likelihood that an IDU partner is already infected is also much higher. Here is a mathematical way to express this phenomenon:

$$P_c = 1 - (1-P_i)^n$$

P_c is the cumulative risk of seroconversion, P_i is the risk of seroconversion from a single risky slip, and n is the number of risky slips. "Slips" are defined as exposure to another person without adequate protection, but "risky slips" are defined as exposure to an *infected* person without adequate protection.

In most parts of the developed world, the prevalence of HCV among IDUs is much higher than that of HIV. In Western Europe, HCV antibody prevalence ranged between 37% and 98% in 66 studies reviewed by Mathei and colleagues ("Seroprevalence of hepatitis C markers among intravenous drug users in western European countries: a systematic review" in *Journal of Viral Hepatitis*, volume 9, 2002). And in San Francisco in 2000, at least 72% of IDUs are HCV antibody positive, while only 10% of them are HIV antibody positive (San Francisco Department of Public Health estimates, December 2000). This means that if an uninfected person has 40 "slips" over several years, and exposes himself to a random selection of IDU partners, something like 30 of those "slips" will be "risky slips" in regard to HCV, but only four or so will be "risky slips" for HIV.

The different values of P_i now come into play. For HIV, the probability (risk) of seroconversion from a single exposure to an infected partner via shared injection works is estimated at one in 150, or .0067. The risk for HCV is much greater (see Appendix), roughly one in 10, or .10. This means that a person who logs 40 "slips" in San Francisco is far more likely to seroconvert to HCV:

$$P_c \text{ for HCV} = 1 - (1 - .10)^{30} = 1 - .042 = .958$$

$$P_c \text{ for HIV} = 1 - (1 - .0067)^{4} = 1 - .967 = .033$$

The estimated probability of seroconversion for HCV is nearly 29 in 30, while that for HIV is only about one in 30.

The approach used here is crude and depends on several simplifying assumptions. Firstly, IDUs don't really select their shooting partners at random; it's plausible that a newly-initiated IDU will have partners who are also newly-initiated, and hence more likely to be HCV-negative. Secondly, "slips" aren't all the same; one user may shake out the proffered works and wipe the needle on his sleeve, possibly reducing infectivity without actual disinfection, while another may use a syringe that's been "registered" (blood drawn in to demonstrate that a vein has been hit) by the first user. Thirdly, IDUs range widely in the frequency with which they "slip": some do so dozens of times a year, while others rarely or never do so in a decade of usage. The former sort get HCV very quickly while the latter sort generally remain uninfected. (This phenomenon is examined in greater detail in the Appendix.)

The above analysis suggests that the outlook for new initiates to injection drug use is dire: if they share uncleaned "works" more than a few times, they're likely to get HCV. But even for those who are always careful with needles, there are risks:

- the "cooker" wherein the drug is dissolved;
- the "cotton" that strains the liquid as it's drawn into the needle;
- the skin surface around the injection site;
- abscesses which may abrade and bleed;
- even for those who don't inject, there are the tubes used for snorting, and the hot glass or metal pipes used in crack-smoking;
- and also shared razors, toothbrushes, tattooing needles, etc.

Of course, for each of these the P_i or risk from single exposure is likely to bc much less than the P_i for needle-sharing. But an IDU may have many, many "low risk" exposures in a year, and is not so likely to be meticulous about disinfecting such trivia as cookers, cottons, or shaving razors.

Problem Two: IDUs Most at Risk Are Hard to Reach

The result of all this is that HCV spreads rapidly among "new" IDUs. Here is what a typical city is likely to see, in terms of HCV infection as a function of length of injection drug using (Lorvick and colleagues, "Prevention and duration of Hepatitis C among injection drug users in San Francisco, Calif." in *American Journal of Public Health*, volume 91, 2001):

Time since first regular injection of drugs	Percent of IDUs infected with HCV
2 years	75% +
4 years	85% +
8 years	95% +

So, most HCV infection occurs in the glorious morning of one's "career" as an injection drug user, not in the troubled noontime or the dreary afternoon. That morning is a time of pleasure and joyful experimentation. The "rush" is fabulous, one still has a job and a back account, one still lives in a decent house or apartment, one still enjoys the trust of friends and family, and as for syringes, well, they can be "loaned" by user friends or "borrowed" from Aunt Millie's diabetic supplies. This means that all the usual places for prevention education– treatment programs, emergency rooms, Narcotics Anonymous or similar Twelve Step programs, the criminal justice system, the inner-city street scene– aren't very relevant for the simple reason that the user *isn't there yet*.

The core problem is that it's hard to find users when they're in the critical early months of their usage. And even if they are found (by diligent outreach workers, for example) prevention is a tough sell for people whose concerns are so much focused on the here and now: they're being asked to act now to prevent potential sickness that's not merely 10 years away, as with AIDS, but 20 or 30 years. Moreover, a friendship network of IDUs may encompass a 10-year span of "user careers", but not a 20- or 30-year span, which means the newest users are likely to know (and be influenced by) someone dealing with AIDS, but they won't know anyone yet "old" enough to have developed liver disease.

Problem Three: The Lack of Self-Help

Often during the 20-year war against HIV disease, initiatives and leadership came from the patients rather than the health professions. With HCV, it's not going to happen, for three reasons:

- No major part of the HCV-infected population is a natural political constituency. The largest proportion of the HIV-infected Americans were gay men, and AIDS hit at the very time they were organizing to gain civil rights and social acceptance. The Pride parades, the Political Action Committees, the fund-raisers, the precinct organizing, the community centers, the gay-oriented media–all could be adapted for the new struggle against HIV. This won't happen for the HCV-infected population, which is heterogeneous and geographically scattered, and much less middle-class than the HIV-infected population was.

• Disease onset happens at a different stage of life than infection. Most people get infected with HCV in young adulthood or earlier. If and when this infection manifests itself as liver disease, they're very different people: middle-aged and far from the people and places among which they'd got infected. The people now hurting from HCV can't connect with those who will be hurting 20 or 30 years from now.

• Most HCV-infected people will never suffer seriously from liver disease. Many will never even know they're infected. So why should they get serious about political activism?

What to Do: Four Long Shots

Genuine HCV prevention requires that an attitude of great caution be an integral part of an injector's life. Use of drugs has to mimic the doctor's office: careful, systematic procedures with alcohol wipes, sterile syringes kept in wrappers until just before use, meticulous disposal, etc. Is there hope to instill such caution into the routine of someone in the honeymoon morning of an injection career? There are at least six hopeful possibilities, but four of them are "long shots":

(1) Hope for a public health leadership that's more worried about what they *don't* do than what they do.
This is a truly long shot. Even such enlightened places as San Francisco were ill-served in the early days of the AIDS epidemic. I was involved in S.F. Department of Public Health discussions in the summer of 1983, when it was clear that an infectious agent was causing a doubling *every six months* in the numbers of ill people. Drastic measures should have been, but were not, contemplated.

Public health leadership was cautious, incremental, and respectful of people's civil rights. What a difference from the great Spanish flu epidemic of 1918! Then, public health leadership was activist, authoritarian, and prompt. A fond (and forlorn) hope is that an Everett Koop will emerge, in San Francisco if not in Washington DC, who will push for Broadcast Education as described below.

(2) Get IDUs to stop injecting.
One way to do this is to provide treatment and recovery programs to attract IDUs away from "the life". Much sincere and costly effort has been made in the past generation to do so, but relapse and new recruitment has kept IDU numbers at a more or less constant level (circa 1.5 million). Another hope is that injected drugs will become so cheap that users can avail themselves of "milder" routes– smoking heroin or opium rather than injecting heroin, drinking coca tea rather than injecting cocaine or speed, et cetera. This hope hasn't played out either, partly because of supply suppression policies and partly because of the natural progression of user "careers".

(3) Hope for a simple technical fix.
The most obvious possibility is a cheap non-reusable syringe, for example one whose barrel can only be drawn "up" once. It is unlikely that a wholesale conversion of syringe technology– with a non-reusable format fully displacing the current reusable format– will occur in the near future. And even if it did, the ingenuity of users may find a way to detach and re-use the needle portion; or they may simply share the contents of a single shot.

(4) Pay people– generously!– for safer behavior.
Many, or most, IDUs who carry the HCV don't know it. But most of them are also chronically short of money. In

view of the costs of future liver disease, it makes sense to offer generous incentives to come in for a HCV screening, and (for those who test positive) to pay them to be educated in "how to protect your partners and loved ones from your disease". This strategy, though sensible epidemiologically, is difficult politically: it's hard to justify giving money "to people who'll just use it to buy more drugs".

What to Do: Two Easier Shots

What's needed is a much higher standard of harm reduction. The nub of the problem is that HCV is very easily transmitted, and therefore most IDUs get infected early on; so prevention has to get to them before they get into the phase of overdoses, arrests, treatment programs, and the hard-core "street scene". The two best hopes are Broadcast Education and Normalized Needle Exchange:

(5) Broadcast Education.
Every young person should be educated about safer parenteral practices, thus to prepare the small minority who will later become drug users. This means that middle school and high school kids have to learn about the perils of drug paraphernalia– and also about the paths to recovery from substance abuse (Twelve Step, treatment programs, et cetera.) In turn, this means that a (small) section has to be added to the health education part of the school curriculum. This will require much patient, diplomatic work in negotiating the political and bureaucratic processes whereby school curricula are modified.

(6) Normalize Needle Exchange.
It is realistic to hope that the inquiry, "Can you tell me where the needle exchange is?" will become as normal as,

"Can you tell me where the methadone program is?" Needle exchange and methadone maintenance are both sensible ways of addressing the problems consequent to drug use. Most US cities with more than a thousand heroin injectors have at least one methadone program; the goal should be that most such cities also have at least one needle exchange site.

Appendix

The estimate of P_i for HIV = .0067 comes from the work of Edward Kaplan and Robert Heimer (Kaplan *et al*, 1994). The estimate of P_i for HCV = .10 comes from an examination of Behavioral Risk Assessment data obtained from San Francisco IDUs in 1998. That sample of IDUs divided roughly into thirds in terms of risk, with the "riskiest third" experiencing five or more "slips" every 90 days, the "middle third" logging one to four slips, and the "safest third" experiencing only one to four slips per year. By assuming that the IDUs in the sample are representative of the S.F. IDU population as a whole, and that they select injection partners at random from a population which is 75% HCV+, the following table can then be generated for three trial values of P_i:

Seroconversion probability after these numbers of slips:

	4	12	40	120
If P_i is .05	.143	.370	.785	(all)
If P_i is .10	.271	.613	.958	(all)
If P_i is .15	.386	.768	(all)	(all)

The trial value of .05 is too small: seroconversion would happen too slowly, especially in the "middle third" to account for the observed prevalence of HCV in San Francisco of at least 72%. Conversely, the trial value of .15 is too large: HCV would sweep through all of that "middle third" and much of the "safest third", and yield a prevalence above 80% even among those with fewer than two years of injection usage. Hence a P_i value of roughly .10 seems best to account for the observed prevalence of HCV.

A similar analysis may explain why we seem to be getting "more than our money's worth" in HIV prevention. The best estimates of risk reduction among IDUs in San Francisco indicates that they're logging about 70% fewer slips now than in 1986, when our prevention campaign began in earnest. But the actual incidence of HIV has dropped by more like 90%: from six seroconversions per 100 person-years in 1986 to 0.6 seroconversions per 100 person-years in 2006. The explanation for this happy state of affairs may simply be this: yes, a minority of HIV-negative IDUs are logging lots of slips, but lots of these high-risk people are *only sharing with HIV-negative partners.* In a city where there's only a one-in-10 chance that an IDU partner is HIV+, it's not hard to be "lucky", even when one is careless about sharing works.

VIII.

The Parable of the Vouchers

Parable VIII.

A Brief History of the After Sobriety Movement

April 2012

San Francisco's After Sobriety movement was inspired by Yvonne Williams, a young crack abuser who in 2004 finally resolved to quit the drug. With the help of a support group of like-minded women, she managed to stay clean, but was frustrated in getting enough help to put her life back together. The critical moment came at a public hearing in the Spring of 2005, when Ms. Williams angrily declared, "we've done our job, we've cleaned up, why can't you help us?...we just can't relate to your treatment programs– give us better choices!" Hearing this, the City's officials were inspired to realize, "My God, *these people possess a commodity which the public is willing to buy.* Why *not* enable them to exchange it on the free market and give them the power of choice?"

That commodity is *sobriety*, a manifest benefit to substance users' families, neighbors, and community, as well as to themselves. The great innovation of the City back in 2005 was to "pay" for this commodity in vouchers– vouchers to use as a medium of exchange by people in recovery.

The After Sobriety movement helped San Francisco to create a new strategy against substance abuse, composed of three parts: self-help "Groups" of people committed to being clean and sober; "Visiting Staff" providing all kinds of services needed "after sobriety"; and the City, regulating and coordinating the whole system.

The Groups

Sobriety groups are the foundation of the system, the bedrock support for abstinence and recovery. There are now more than a thousand such groups. There are Native American groups, teenage groups, senior citizen groups, ex-con groups, computer-nerd groups, Salvadoran refugee groups, Laotian groups, even a "leathermen stockbrokers" group. Many formed by slow accretion of friends and acquaintances, many found their members through the Internet, some were organized by psychotherapists, some simply arose from the culture of the streets. Many groups operate on Twelve Step principles, others are frankly Christian or Muslim, still others are simply rap groups. Some meet every day, some only once a week; the average is three or four meetings per week. Some are as small as nuclear families, others have nearly 100 members; the average size is 12. But all the groups share one thing: a conviction that substance abuse is destructive, and that abstinence is the only real hope. A few of the groups permit themselves a little beer or wine, but most commit to avoiding *all* intoxicating substances, legal or illicit.

The "culture of honesty" is absolutely central to the groups' identity. Honesty is *the* paramount cultural virtue; as Yvonne Williams puts it, "Better a truthful old White guy than a lying sister!" Group participants are razor-sharp– and ruthless– at detecting lies or "slips". And because the groups offer things of great value quite apart from the vouchers– friendship, intimacy, and community– their participants are motivated to adhere to the norm of sobriety, much more so than they would be in any treatment program.

With the help of Project Open Hand, the groups are able to

nurture their participants in a quite basic way: delicious hot meals at most of the meetings. Generous support from the City enabled Open Hand to adapt to the decline of HIV-related needs, and start serving a different population. These meals have proved to be *very* valuable morale boosters.

In the Groups, people learned to like and trust one another. This has enabled a great many of them to team up and rent large apartments and flats, sharing costs. By thus forming "extended families of choice" to obtain housing, one pressing problem of "how do we get our lives together, after sobriety?" has been largely solved. But what about the many other needs of people beginning lives in recovery? These needs are addressed by Vouchers.

The After Sobriety Visiting Staff

Beginning in 2008, the City issued "After Sobriety Vouchers" to all participants of registered groups. These vouchers could be freely exchanged for a wide variety of needed services:

- Vocational counseling
- Psychological counseling
- Stress reduction counseling
- Urban life skills counseling
- Medical care
- Childcare
- Adult education

More than a thousand "After Sobriety Visiting Staff" are now registered to provide these services. The "Visiting Staff" are just that: they come to the clients, rather than waiting for the clients to come to them. Their middle-class traits of owning cars, keeping appointments, being on time, etc., suit them well for their work: most of it consists of arriving at an appointed time (usually the end of a scheduled group meeting) to provide services to the group members, either collectively or individually. For these services the Visiting Staff are given vouchers, which they can in turn exchange for something of value: salaries and fringe benefits. The more vouchers earned, the higher the salary.

The Vouchers quickly solved the problem of cultural competency: if you weren't able to relate to the folks in a group, you weren't invited back. Those that were competent at least with some groups, thrived. Visiting Staff annual earnings range up to $100,000, and up to $150,000 for physicians. Surprisingly, the most successful have been middle-aged Latinas, who are particularly in demand by groups of young men struggling to overcome "speed" abuse. In the early days of After Sobriety, these women were so in demand that they made *big* money, but eventually the supply increased to meet the demand.

The morale of the Visiting Staff is generally high. Especially attractive is the variety and challenge of the tasks, and the flexibility to work as many or as few hours as desired. Even the physicians enjoy a role reminiscent of the traditional family doctor, carrying his black bag and making house calls...

The City's Role

The City's main jobs, through its Internet Substance Abuse Systems (ISAS) office, are to keep a registry of groups, to run the vouchers system, and to certify the basic skills of the Visiting Staff. The City also provides space, free of charge, in its buildings for the groups' meetings. Finally, the City regularly monitors the system to expand the parts that are working and redesign the parts that are not.

Moneys to pay for the vouchers system originally came from the City's substance abuse treatment funding. As treatment program staff quit to register for the more lucrative and enjoyable Visiting Staff jobs, and as clients deserted for the more relevant sobriety groups, the City's treatment programs gradually atrophied and shut down, thus freeing funding. But the huge success of the new system required more funds. Beginning in 2008, these were raised by City taxes on alcohol and tobacco, amounting to about 12 dollars per quart of whisky, and a dollar per pack of cigarettes. After marijuana was legalized in 2010, it too was taxed. Polls show that the San Francisco citizenry is pleased that "substance users are paying the downstream costs of their abuse". There is currently a lot of pressure to regulate cocaine, heroin, and other drugs so that they, too, can provide tax revenue; but so far the only real revenue these drugs provide to the vouchers program is through seizure of drug traffickers' assets. Even so, the system will operate at a net gain to the City in Fiscal Year 2013: $77 million will be raised in alcohol, tobacco, and marijuana taxes, but the voucher system and its administration will only cost $68 million.

An Overview

In retrospect, we failed to predict back in 2007 how quickly San Francisco's substance abuse strategy would be renewed by the system described above. We expected a lot of resistance from entrenched interests, but it just evaporated. The line staff of the treatment programs jumped at the opportunity to escape the stifling confines and endless paperwork of "The Program" and go freelance. The program executives were at first resistant, but soon realized that they too could redefine their work: now they specialize in harm reduction outreach to the (smaller but still sizable) population of abusers not in recovery. As for the San Francisco Police Department, it grudgingly agreed with Brendan Behan that

> There is no manifestation
> of addictive disease
> That cannot be made worse
> by the involvement
> of a police officer

and was thankful for a new climate in which substance use was mostly decriminalized.

Had we, 10 years ago, reflected on the worldwide failure of centrally planned *economies*, we might have realized, as we do now, that centrally planned *social service systems* are also inclined to fail. We began to sense something was wrong during the 2003 public hearings on "Treatment on Demand", which became so mired in a tangled swamp of internal contradictions, reams of information, and "huge needs everywhere". It took the cry for empowerment of a young Black woman to focus us on the greatest need of people in recovery: consumer choice in a free market.

Commentary

The above Parable is meant to provoke us to consider the private sector as a provider of recovery services. The free market is a wonderful arbiter of value: the "invisible hand" directs resources to where they're needed and wanted, so that what works for people flourishes, and what doesn't work atrophies. The great pitfall with free-market mechanisms in healthcare, as Paul Krugman points out, is that providers love to care for the healthiest, and love to exclude the sickest from their care. For this reason, it's important that the substance abuse treatment sector has a "single payer", empowered to cover all care costs for all comers.

As conceived in my Parable, that "single payer" is government– government acting on the principles of "legalize, tax, regulate, discourage" and "tax sufficiently to cover the downstream costs". Thus the "downstream costs" of alcohol include all the expenses of treating those individuals who– despite the tax-influenced high cost of booze, despite the regulations against underage use, despite the campaigns to discourage alcohol abuse– still manage to get in trouble with alcohol. Whatever tax is required to cover these downstream costs, the consumer must meet it, just as consumers of coal ought to be required to meet the downstream (i.e. environmental) costs of coal exploitation. These taxes may be high– $120 per gallon of pure alcohol is about right to cover those downstream costs– but they have the double benefit of discouraging use and of enhancing the tolerance of non-users.

Once the huge pot of tax moneys are available within an open, free market environment, there will be no shortage of providers bidding for business, just as with the

Pentagon bidding out to private providers. What remains is to provide sufficient regulation to prevent abuses, to assure fair competition, and to protect the consumer against fraud.

Save Many Trees But Lose the Forest: The Paradox of Drug Treatment

Background. From the perspective of drug treatment programs and their clients, a lot of good is obviously being done. Whether it's methadone maintenance, residential treatment, or outpatient drug-free, many success stories can be cited. The turnaround in people's lives is beautiful and poignant. Moreover, it's cost-effective: with as few as 20 true success stories in a million-dollar program, the program will reach its "quota" and pay for itself– and many programs can document many times their "quota".

Hypothesis. The paradox is that, from society's point of view, all this good work is just a drop in the bucket– or, more precisely, a pint in a gallon. The problem is the scale of drug treatment: there needs to be about eight times as much. It's not just that there are chronically too few slots for "treatment on demand", but also that the treatment programs mostly fall woefully short of providing the thoroughgoing help (better housing conditions, psychotherapy, couples therapy, jobs) that people need. So from the user's point of view, a drug treatment program is merely an occasional comfort station along a decades-long career path of addiction.

Testing the Hypothesis. Obtain a random sample of citizens in their 50s who are in recovery (i.e., abstinent) after prolonged addiction. Then do in-depth interviews around the question, "What were the things that helped you begin a life in recovery?" If "treatment programs" comprise only 10% or 15% of the aggregate list of things, my hypothesis is essentially proven.

A Radical Suggestion. Obviously local, state and Federal governments should "invest" many times more in treatment, because the return on investment will be huge. San Francisco's Treatment on Demand task force strove mightily to achieve this multifold increase, as have many other well-meaning task forces.

Very little has changed. Why? The short answer is that government bodies in general lack the vision to "invest" wisely.

My radical proposal is to privatize drug treatment. Entrepreneurs would "invest" by providing the services they judge to be most cost-effective to the target populations. Return on investment would be in proportion to outcomes: the greater the decline in substance abuse (and in property crimes, joblessness, domestic violence, and other blights associated with substance abuse) the greater the profits. One easily measured outcome would be the increase in property values in a neighborhood where drug-abuse blights disappear. Increased property values translate to increased property tax collections; that increase could be passed on to the entrepreneurs as a reward for their investment– i.e., the City/County of San Francisco would pass on its increased revenue to the private funders of drug treatment.

The City/County government needs to be involved to assure that entrepreneurs give at least as much attention to poor neighborhoods as to rich ones. This is where "vouchers" can play a key role: each citizen diagnosed with addictive disease receives an annual supply of vouchers, exchangeable for relevant treatment services. These vouchers comprise a significant economic incentive for providers who can cash them in. Because addictive disease diagnoses are (somewhat) more common in poor neighborhoods, those areas will be better served by the service-providing entrepreneurs.

In the future as much as in the past, abstinence support groups of the Twelve Step sort may prove to be the most cost-efficient treatment modality. Thus it may well be that churches in low-SES districts are the greatest beneficiaries of the voucher system. It shouldn't be hard to initiate a virtuous circle: a church provides free space for Twelve Step meetings; the attendees give their vouchers to the church; the church exchange the vouchers for work to keep their facilities in good repair; the better-maintained church attracts more members, including recovering abusers; and so forth.

IX.

The Parable of Policy Reversal

Parable IX.

The Institute for Policy Negation

by Fr. Ignatius Newmeyer

I have observed that public policies, despite the good intentions with which they are conceived and executed, often leave the world *worse* off. Some arenas seem particularly prone to unintended and unhappy policy consequences:

- Welfare programs for the poor
- Military interventions
- Promoting agriculture in marginal lands
- "Improving" the lot of indigenous peoples
- Controlling substance use

I know a lot about the last of these: I've been responsible for 30 years for monitoring the level of use of illicit drugs in San Francisco. In those years, huge amounts of taxpayer money were spent to urge people to avoid drugs, to arrest dealers, to interdict drug importation, and to destroy crops on the ground. In spite of these heroic efforts, three of the four major drugs (heroin, cocaine, and "speed") now cost less on the street, and are more widely used, than in 1980. Only marijuana costs more and is used less than 25 years ago. The question naturally arises, "Would we be better off now if *no* substance use control policies had been devised and carried out?" And if we dare to think the answer might be "yes", what can we do in the future to prevent ill-fated policies from being launched?

The problem is that, in substance use as in so many other arenas, the advantage lies with those who are eager to *do something*. We Americans are persistently hopeful that our condition can be improved through planning. Our mayors, legislators, and social science faculties have a can-do attitude. So we send immigrants to plow the future Dust Bowl, we build high-rise public housing monstrosities fated for dynamiting, and we send half a million citizens to prison for no other crime than peddling feel-good substances. Always there have been doubters, but always they lacked the esprit and institutional cohesion of the boosters. But maybe, just maybe...

Herewith an account of the creation of an academy dedicated to *resisting* policy implementation, namely the **Institute for Policy Negation**. Its Latin motto is *Considerate Nihil Agere* ("Consider doing nothing", or as many wryly put it, "Leave it the **** alone!") The Institute has a Jesuit form: bright, ambitious men and women enter a four-year advanced-level program to hone their skills in analysis, debate, and communication. Each I.P.N. graduate is meant to become splendidly able to fudge, delay, negotiate, and compromise. They learn the arts of organizing resistance among people affected by policy initiatives, of "questioning the need for this program", of "further study is needed". They become masters at generating public anxiety about "hidden costs", "unintended consequences", "the loss of what we hold dear", and so forth. Most of all, each graduate strives to achieve the knack of yielding– if yield he must– with a thunderous, "I demand future accounting for the extravagant use of taxpayer dollars upon which we are about to embark!" The graduate is individually responsible to monitor this accounting– but that role is backed by the institutional memory of the I.P.N. to assure that the architects of failed policies, and their disciples, are hounded by blame and ridicule *for decades* after the event.

Institute for Policy Negation graduates have a distinctive personal style not unlike Jesuits: skeptical, caustic, world-weary, but open to fleshly pleasures and laughter. That style contrasts with the earnest, optimistic, but somewhat naive personal style of the policy enthusiasts. And the enthusiasts have come to expect their opponents to appear ("I rise to challenge the rosy assumptions of Dr. — !") in setpiece battles as routine in 21st Century America as Democrat-Republican confrontations in the 20th Century.

I.P.N. graduates do not automatically reject all policy initiatives, yielding gracefully in many an arena– public health outreach to children, for example. But even there, there is a tone of hesitation and skepticism.

The **Institute for Policy Negation** is an adjunct of Yale University. In New Haven, I.P.N. students and faculty have the salutary experience of living amidst the evidence of countless failed social science schemes to "improve" the town and its people.

Other nations are now in the process of creating their own versions of the Institute– in France, an "École Normale de Nonadministration", and in Britain, a Melbourne College within the Oxford University system, wherein students can master the style of Prime Minister Melbourne:

To promise, pause, prepare, postpone
And end by letting things alone:
In short, to earn the people's pay
By doing nothing every day.

Affirmative Inaction

American drug abuse policy in the last generation has been an almost unbroken series of disasters. The full story of these policy failures is too complex to enumerate in this short essay, but the general themes have been *cruelty* and *waste*. Perhaps the most cruel and wasteful disaster has been the impact on Black Americans. Many hundreds of thousands of these citizens have been harassed, intimidated, arrested, incarcerated, disenfranchised, and generally made miserable, solely because of their usage and/or selling of illicit drugs.

As with many another policy disaster, there were good intentions. It seemed reasonable that vigorous law enforcement against drug trafficking and usage would destroy the market and discourage Black people from using. The big problem– aside from the fact that the effort has failed and people use drugs as much as ever– is that Blacks have borne *far more than their share* of the impact of law enforcement. If we learned anything from the "Greatest Generation" that fought and won the Second World War, it is that burdens and sacrifices must be shared fairly, if America is truly to live up to its values.

Therefore, I propose a policy of **Fairness in Sentencing**, or "Affirmative Inaction", whereby all races will, at last, fairly share the sacrifices needed to suppress drug trafficking and usage.

We apply affirmative action policies to ensure that college admissions are as racially diverse as the youth population. Different admission standards are applied to Blacks, in the belief that their lower high school grades and SAT scores reflect past disadvantages and discrimination rather than inferior innate intelligence. Just as we *augment* the flow of Blacks into colleges, we should *diminish* the flow of Blacks into the criminal justice system, for the same noble goal of racial justice. Just as we even out the opportunities for future privilege (via college admissions), we should even out the risks for future problems (via drug busts).

Let me illustrate how this would work, using cocaine as an example. Thanks to the National Household Survey, we have a fairly accurate idea of how racial groups are apportioned among cocaine users: in 2004, 62% of current cocaine users were Whites, 24% were Blacks, 12% were Latinos, and 2% were Asians or other races. These proportions reflect the true share of Americans' responsibility for its cocaine problem, for surely we agree that all users are complicit in that problem, whether they are buyers or sellers; this principle applies in prostitution, where "johns" as well as prostitutes are targeted by law enforcement. These, then, are our target quotas for enforcement of the laws against cocaine use and trafficking: we will strive toward a prison population whose cocaine-law incarcerants are 62% White, 24% Black, and 12% Latino.

Of course most drug-law enforcement is at the state or local level, so we need to apply NHS or other surveys to determine the state or local proportions of cocaine use by race, thus to set the State or local quotas. Then a statute of Mandatory Probation can be applied: if a judge has a cocaine-law conviction of an individual, and if the incarceration of that individual would exceed the quota for that person's racial group, then the judge would be mandated to issue a sentence of probation rather than incarceration. So, just as we have tied judges' hands through Mandatory Sentencing statutes, we will tie judges' hands through Mandatory Probation.

The effect of Mandatory Probation statutes would be that Blacks convicted of cocaine offenses would be diverted to probation, while Whites thus convicted could be incarcerated without limit, until the White proportion of the coke-bust prison population was finally beefed up to the proper level. For the considerable time required for this "beefing up", White cocaine users would feel an unaccustomed degree of hassling, but (if we believe that police action discourages drug use) this could have the salutary effect of suppressing demand. The suppression of demand would lead to a decline in the profits of drug lords and perhaps a lessening of terrorism in Colombia and other places. Therefore, the new Mandatory Probation statutes could be introduced as part of a larger "Suppression of Terrorism" policy initiative.

Admittedly, the concept of Mandatory Probation, the key to the whole approach of Affirmative Inaction, is a novelty and a tough sell. California may have to lead the way in this, just as it did with tougher emission controls, banning of tobacco smoking in public places, Proposition 36, and much else. California bears the same relation to the Federal Government as a clever student does to an unprepared, befuddled professor: sometimes the student just has to take over the class for awhile.

A major criticism of Mandatory Probation is that it would give Black Americans a "holiday" from cocaine-law prosecution. To which we can reply: the Black community deserves such a holiday to make up for their past excess burden of such prosecution. And anyway, if Blacks increased their cocaine usage as a result of this "holiday", this would soon be reflected in NHS and other data, which in turn would enable quotas to be re-set to allow increased prosecution of Blacks.

Sick and Poor, Sick and Rich

In his book, *Unhealthy Societies: The Afflictions of Inequality*, Richard Wilkinson shows that health is directly related to social class: the nearer you are to the bottom of the social ladder, the sicker you are likely to be and the younger you are likely to die. If you're poor, you leave school earlier, you have children earlier, your organs wear out earlier, and you grow old before your time. Television, smoking, and alcohol are about the only kinds of recreation you can afford. When you're sick, you'll wait a long time to see a doctor who'd probably prefer working elsewhere. Added to these obvious consequences of poverty, Wilkinson argues, are two less tangible factors that augment the disadvantage of the poor: higher stress and lesser social cohesion.[1]

To illustrate these "Afflictions of Inequality", let's contrast "Harry", a rich American from a rich family, with "Bill", a man poor all his life, as each copes with HIV infection. There are many ways in which Harry is better

---

1 The role of stress in health was elucidated in a decades-long followup study of 18,000 male British civil servants. It was found that the lowest employment grades had four times the rate of heart attacks as the highest, apparently because "lack of control in one's workplace" results in higher stress. The importance of social cohesion was demonstrated in a study of Italian immigrants and their descendants in Roseto, Pennsylvania. The first generation, in spite of a diet of rich traditional foods, had heart attacks at half the U.S. rate. Later generations, having "assimilated" into American patterns– and away from tight-knit Italian community traditions– had heart attacks at the usual U.S. rate.

off:

<u>Harry has much more money than Bill</u>

He can pay his own medical bills if need be. He can also travel far in pursuit of just the right doctor or pharmacy.

Harry can have people do tasks that would otherwise run down his energies. He can hire maids, send out his laundry, and order in his meals.

Harry can buy things that directly impact his health, such as protein-rich foods, filtered water, and vitamins. He can also furnish his life with things that indirectly affect health through stress reduction or morale enhancement, for example a good stereo system, cable TV, flowers, and nice clothes. Harry can also afford to keep in touch with distant friends– or HIV experts– by regular long-distance phone calls.

Bill has no access to credit or even a credit card. Harry's resources are vast, even compared to the $200,000 or more it may cost him to battle HIV disease for a lifetime.

Bill is obliged to spend most of his time near where he lives. Harry, if he wants, can take vacations just about whenever and wherever.

When Bill travels around town, he's much more reliant on public transportation, with all of its attendant stresses and (especially in winter) communicable diseases. Harry can drive his own (well-maintained) car or use cabs.

Harry lives in a nicer neighborhood

His home is quiet and "healing". He has more living space, which is cleaner because he hires people to keep it so. If he must maintain a complex 30-pill-per-day HIV medications regimen, his living space– clocks, refrigerators, privacy, etc.– will be conducive.

Bill lives in a more dangerous neighborhood, which inhibits even such daily routines as taking a walk or going to the neighborhood store. And at the store, the reception is wary and the prices high. Some of the neighbors have a notorious tendency to prey upon the weak. All this adds to stress.

Bill's home is much more likely to be invaded by burglars, or by cops impatiently pursuing drug dealers.

The hospitals and clinics in Harry's neighborhood are better. The wait for care is shorter, the waiting rooms are pleasanter, and the staff treat the patients more respectfully.

Harry has had more education, at better schools

He can read and understand the labels and other literature pertinent to his HIV medications.

Thanks to his superior education, Harry is better able to beguile the tedium of long bedridden days by reading, listening to music, conversing with friends, or just thinking. Bill is much more dependent on television.

Harry is far likelier than Bill to own a computer with

Internet access, and to know how to use it to search worldwide for HIV-related treatment information.

Bill is susceptible to "miracle cures", and also to paranoid ideas along the lines of, "AIDS is a CIA plot against the poor". Harry has a healthy skepticism about such things.

Harry is much more aware of the history of human diseases and of his role in that history.

<u>Harry's friends are mostly rich and well-educated, like him, while Bill's friends are mostly poor and badly-educated, like him</u>

Harry has a lot of people from whom he can borrow money if need be.

Harry is also able to borrow quiet spaces for healing, for example a friend's home in the country.

Harry can learn about HIV meds, and even be given them, by friends who are knowledgeable about HIV. Harry may even have several friends who are themselves physicians.

Bill's friends are far more likely to have irrational or paranoid ideas about HIV, healthcare, doctors, and suchlike. The stories he hears from them only exacerbate his anxiety and hopelessness.

<u>Nowadays, bourgeois culture is healthier than proletarian culture</u>

Bill's diet consists of too much fatty foods, and too few

green vegetables and fruits. Even if Bill wanted fresh fruits and vegetables, the stores near his home don't stock them.

Bill gets much less exercise than Harry.

Harry relates to his family and friends in a more healthful, functional way, possibly because they have hired psychiatrists, counselors, family therapists, etc., to work through problems.

Harry's belief in his own personal efficacy is far greater than Bill's.

Bourgeois culture plans for the future. Thus Harry is far better able than Bill to envision the world 10 years hence, and to see himself in it.

Bill has had more brutalizing experiences– fights, crimes, family abuse, hunger, unemployment, classism, perhaps racism. The social cohesion of his neighborhood steadily deteriorates, while Harry's world is, if anything, becoming more cohesive.

Bill can't handle stress as well as Harry: he feels he has minimal control over the stressor, he lacks social support to deal with the stress, and he interprets stress as a sign that things are getting worse and worse.

If Bill's HIV disease is compounded by addiction to an illicit substance, he must face the additional problems of dangerous trafficking, contaminated drugs, police hassles, and perhaps imprisonment. If Harry is addicted, he's likelier to have a "cleaner" connection for his drugs, and his bourgeois status assures kinder treatment by cops and judges.

Commentary: What Is To Be Done?

From this long and melancholy listing, it is obvious that a poor person fighting HIV disease is hugely disadvantaged, in terms of stress and social cohesion as well as the more obvious factors of wealth, education, and living environment. Moreover, the proportion of "Bills" among Americans living with HIV is now more than one in three, while the proportion of "Harrys" has dropped since 1985 from about 6% to about 2%.

What is to be done? First off, we should reexamine the data to see if what is true for other diseases is also true for HIV. Our hypothesis would be:

> HIV-infected people of high socioeconomic status (SES) have more favorable outcomes of their HIV disease than those of low SES, other factors being equal.

I predict that the data will show that the poor are much worse off than the rich. If so, the most obvious remedy would be a social revolution resulting in redistribution of wealth and genuine equality of opportunity. But this is not in the cards; I expect to grow old and simple, like Mother Jones, in fruitless waiting for that glorious day. Nonetheless, there are important ways in which we can intervene to help the poor face HIV as if they were rich. A superb "system of care" has largely achieved this in San Francisco, mostly by allocating resources– nutritious meals, competent primary care, good information, mental-health services, home care, etc.– directly to the needy. Perhaps that city's system of care would be even better if it also set lower stress and better social cohesion as service goals. To that end, I offer these hypotheses:

HIV+ people who consistently attend Twelve Step groups will have more favorable outcomes of HIV disease than those not in such groups, other factors (SES, etc.) being equal.

HIV+ people who live in intentional communities (e.g., Delancey Street) or in extended families will have more favorable outcomes than those who live alone, other factors being equal.

HIV+ people who are involved in communities of faith, such as Glide Memorial Church, will have more favorable outcomes than those not thus involved, other factors being equal.

HIV+ first-generation Latino immigrants will have more favorable outcomes than second- or third-generation Latino-Americans, other factors being equal.

HIV+ people who consistently deal with stress by medication (such as Prozac) or other methods (such as meditation) will have more favorable outcomes than those who don't deal with their stress, other factors being equal.

HIV+ people who live in rural areas will have more favorable outcomes than those who live in the inner city, other factors (especially isolation and loneliness) being equal.

If research supports some or all of these hypotheses, it will show the way toward further improvements in San Francisco's system of care– and help the thousands of HIV+ Bills in our City to cope more successfully with their infection.

Improving the care of HIV+ people points the way to improving the care of substance abusers: it come down to *more community, more connection.*

Blood on Their Hands: The Judgment of History

A lower-class thief steals a thousand dollars worth of property, and– if caught and convicted three times for such theft– is punished by 25 years in a nasty and brutal penitentiary.

A middle-class savings and loan exploiter defrauds a million dollars from the depositors, and– if caught at it and very unlucky– is punished by a few years in a minimum-security prison.

But what punishment awaits a ruling-class policymaker, whose bad decisions cost the taxpaying public a billion dollars– or thousands of human lives?

Usually, none whatsoever. A sterling example is General Douglas Haig, who commanded British armies in the murderous trench warfare of World War One. After the War, he was raised to the peerage and given a grant of £100,000; upon his death in 1928, he was accorded national tributes to his memory at Westminster Abbey.

Another example is Robert McNamara, the chief architect of the U.S. role in the Vietnam War. Despite doubts that (as he later admitted) began in 1965, he carried on the war with increased intensity, only resigning late in 1967 after billions more dollars and thousands more lives had been squandered. He went on to prestigious employment running the World Bank, and then a comfortable retirement.

The only "punishment" for Haig and McNamara and their ilk is the savage judgment of History. Of Haig the official view (*Encyclopedia Britannica*, 1974) now reads, "...his strategies of attrition (tautly summarized as 'kill more Germans') resulted in enormous numbers of British casualties but little immediate gain in 1916-17." An even more caustic view of McNamara is gradually emerging as the history of the Vietnam War era is written.

It is embittering to realize that the egregious decision-makers who stymied needle exchange and bleach-and-teach for so long– I am resisting the temptation to name names here– will enjoy lives like Haig's and McNamara's. They'll keep their jobs, and even be promoted or re-elected.

At least we are beginning to write the shameful history of the early years of the war against HIV. Our revenge, for what it's worth, will be History's judgment, summarized in the enduring metaphor of "blood on their hands." But perhaps History's judgment can be *accelerated* a bit, with IPN graduates (see p. 130) hounding and heckling the perpetrators in their later lives...

X.

The Parable of the Mildstuff

Parable X.

A Short History of the Conquest of the Crack Epidemic

It all started on that sunny spring morning four years ago. There had been yet another police sweep of Bayview's Third Street corridor the night before, with 40 young men hauled off to jail on charges of trafficking in crack cocaine. As always, these same youths would be back on the street in a day or two, selling their potent wares just as before – but meanwhile, there was no one offering the stuff, and there were dozens of jittery, unhappy buyers milling about on the corners or sulking in their cars. It was at that moment, at about 10:30 AM on Wednesday, April 18, 2007, that the "Prevention Pot" program made its appearance on Third Street and on the pages of our city's history.

At first no one knew what to make of the Prevention Pot women– they seemed to appear out of nowhere, carrying big old-fashioned metal coffeepots, approaching the knots of frustrated crack buyers with their singsong, "Hey, honey, you lookin' awful– try a cup of this nice hot tea!" It didn't take long for the word to get around that their tea was *good*. By noon all the anxious crackheads along a one-mile stretch of Third Street had tried at least one cup of this aromatic green drink, and they found that they were no longer jittery, but instead had a warm glow of calm self-confidence arising from the very pit of their stomachs. The Prevention Pot people disappeared for a few hours, but they were back for another hour in the late afternoon, and again for awhile in the late evening. By day's end, their styrofoam cups had replaced "crack" vials as the most telltale litter of Third Street.

Prevention Pot was back on Thursday– some new faces, but again mostly big, middle-aged women with nurturing, friendly manners, and still wielding those distinctive big blue enamel coffeepots. Somehow there was enough tea for everyone. That evening, several of the crack dealers returned to the street, only to find most of their former customers feeling just *fine* behind their cups of green tea, and not in the market for "hubbas". The dealers grumbled a lot, but dared do nothing against these matronly women– one even recognized his own *grandma*. They took their commerce to the more accepting markets of Ingleside and Visitacion Valley.

It took several more days before the S.F. Police Department realized what was happening: Prevention Pot's hot green tea was nothing less than a brew of coca leaves! The SFPD made preparations to bust Prevention Pot, whose routine of "working" Third Street for an hour each morning, afternoon, and evening had by now become familiar. But a patrolman pointed out that calls from the Third Street area had dropped by 60% since the 18th. The SFPD, ever one to "let sleeping dogs lie", decided to hold off for awhile.

By the end of Summer 2007, the "good women of Third Street" had become familiar and respected figures in the neighborhood. Crackheads from other parts of the City came to sample their soothing but invigorating brew; the crack trade in those outlying neighborhoods began to decline. Mayor Newsom extended his approval and protection; the *Chronicle* wrote glowing stories; Channel Four did many an interview for its Six O'Clock News. One TV newsman, David Belvis, coined the now-famous word "cokee" to describe the tea.

The further history of cokee in San Francisco is well known, and will not be belabored here. Probably the most remarkable facet of that history is how quickly the "cokeeshop" phenomenon developed in the City, after the state decriminalized coca leaf in October 2008. Everyone assumed that the crack dealers would fight to regain their market, but they just seemed to disappear in the face of the combined force of community sentiment, continued police pressure, a certain amount of vigilant Guardian Angel activity, and all those persistent, cheery women who seemed so much like people's fussy, caring grandmas...

Sociologists have commented on the amazing turnaround in the quality of life for San Francisco's Black population in recent years. Some say the cause was the near-total replacement of snorted or smokeable cocaine (30 to 90% purity) by coca-leaf tea (.01% cocaine content), and the elimination of criminal trafficking in that substance. There are now more than 200 cokeeshops, selling an average of 500 to 600 cups per day at the regulated price of $2 per cup. The majority of the establishments are in the southeast quarter of the City. The typical proprietor is Black, male, and young; many are former crack dealers. Some observers have commented on the strong resemblance of the San Francisco cokeeshop to the Parisian working-class bistro: the marble tables, the tasty snacks, the tuneful music, the lively banter of the *patron*, the easygoing ambience. But the role of the cokeeshop in restoring the fiscal health of San Francisco also deserves mention: with the tax of $1 per cup, the City grossed more than $35,000,000 in revenues from this source in 2009. As only $12,000,000 was spent on regulating the cokeeshops and funding substance use prevention programs, enough was left to cut the City's deficit in half.

Of course, the tax picture for other drugs has changed, too, since 2007: the application of the Koop Rule (that all substances should be taxed in proportion to the amount of social and health problems they lead to) now means that liquor is taxed at an average of $20 per bottle, and cigarettes at $10 per pack. This has led to a big decrease in the abuse of alcohol and nicotine in all poor communities.

Things were also helped by the Infrastructure Rehabilitation Act of 2009. Sixty billion dollars of defense spending was redirected to the rebuilding of the nation's highways, bridges, sewers, streets, and public housing. A million jobs were created– with San Francisco getting more than its share, thanks to the clout of its Congresswomen. The work was hard and gritty, but it paid well– with overtime and productivity bonuses, as much as $1,500/week– and the muscular young people who thronged the cokeeshops of Bayview and Hunters Point at 7 every morning seemed eager to get to it, after their customary "cuppas".

It seems that the U.S.'s new emphasis on strengthening the family as a healthy economic unit has also made a difference for Black Americans– especially such get-tough legislation as the Mandatory Child Support Law ("miss a payment, go to prison"). And one musn't overlook the recent reforms in banking policies which enabled residents of public housing to buy their apartments (more fully described in "The Condo-ization of Sunnydale", *San Francisco Chronicle,* November 15, 2008).

It took less than eight months for coca-leaf tea to displace crack in San Francisco. No one would have predicted this a scant five years ago. Perhaps these quotes can help explain the phenomenon:

"Sure, crack gives a big high– for about five minutes!", says ex-user Jerry Fowler. "But a couple of cups of cokee holds me all morning, with no messing with my head or *craving*. I can go to work behind it, and there's no more worry about missing my connection. Cokee gives me my money's worth– like, I'd rather have a premium beer than a shot of rotgut whisky."

'Dexter', an ex-convict who now owns a cokeeshop on Third Street, states, "Yeah, I made a lot of money dealing hubbas. I also got totally stressed out from all the hassling by cops. Look, my cafe is going to clear 100 thou this year. I get to keep all this, and I get respect from the community– from the elders as well as the players, and that means a lot to me nowadays!"

"Crack was destroying our Black community, but it would have been much worse if we'd fought it with the fascistic measures some of my colleagues were proposing back in 2005– sometimes the cure is worse than the disease!", declares County Supervisor Naomi White. "I'd just as soon see our young people not using any substances at all– but meanwhile, it's good to see that 60% decrease in Black-on-Black violence, and those tax revenues from the cokeeshops are mighty nice to see, too."

"Coca tea probably saved a thousand black lives in San Francisco", says Tom Coates, author of *Leadership From Below: Two Decades of Public Policy on AIDS* (St. Martin's Press, 2007). "If the level of promiscuous sexual activity associated with crack abuse had continued for even a couple of years longer, the AIDS virus would have spread a lot further than it did."

"I'm less worried about the long-term medical effects of

coca leaf consumption, now that those statistics on Bolivian Indians are in", declares Dr. David Smith, medical director emeritus of the Haight-Ashbury Free Clinic. "They actually live slightly longer than comparable groups of peasants who don't consume the leaf. However, I'm still concerned about the possibility of urinary tract irritation and higher rates of stomach cancer– we need to start some good 30-year longitudinal studies."

Among the very few dissenters from this chorus of approval for coca tea is Dr. John Newmeyer, epidemiologist at the Haight-Ashbury Free Clinic. He states, "It was the turnaround in social and economic policies that made the difference for inner-city people, not the legalization of coca leaf. We don't need another legal psychoactive substance– don't we have enough of them with alcohol, nicotine, caffeine, sugar, and Valium? What we needed five years ago was programs that would have improved the economy of the inner cities, and given people hope and opportunity."

From Strong and Illicit to Mild and Legal: The Ten Advocacies

This chapter's Parable is a straightforward argument that, just possibly, a strong and harmful drug can be replaced by a mild alternative. I've woven several notions into the Parable to show how the odds can be tipped in favor of the "mildstuff":

- The milder form has the same essential psychoactive ingredient (cocaine) as the stronger form. All but one of the Big Eight psychoactive drugs can easily be offered in milder forms, for example heroin as laudanum, marijuana as "homegrown", tobacco in filtered cigarettes, alcohol as beer or wine, caffeine as coffee that's more brown than black, and sugar as a little honey rather than a lot of HFCS. "Speed" is the only drug lacking an obvious mild alternative.

- The coca tea is much closer to the organic form than is "crack". As such, it provides the user with other alkaloids from the coca leaf which might have a psychoactive effect or at least a pleasant taste. Likewise, the winegrape provides tasty esters as well as ethyl alcohol.

- Coca tea is a refreshing beverage, and as such can become part of a mealtime ritual much like one's morning coffee. Mealtime often means other people, who just might provide a framework for controlled use of the substance.

- In the Parable, market forces act in favor of the

mildstuff– the coca tea becomes available as $2 cups, regulated by the City to insure reasonable quality control, and available most of the time at lots of "bistros". The $2 price commends itself to low-income people who often *simply don't have* $10 for a vial of crack.

- In the Parable, the cops hassle the crack dealers but mostly leave the coca tea ladies and the coca tea bistros alone. The reason is obvious: people behave worse under the influence of hard stuff, and dealers fight more in an unregulated, high-profit market.

- The tax revenues from the coca bistros help to assuage the concerns of the rest of the citizenry. Those revenues pay for regulation of the bistros and for public-information campaigns to discourage excess use and use by children.

This tenth and final Parable, then, offers all the aspects of the "Legalize, Tax, Regulate, Discourage" strategy for resolution of our country's substance abuse problems. I believe the strategy is useful for all of the Big Eight substances but one (see "Consuming Passions", page 3, and "Speed Exceptionalism", page 61).

The *strategy* is straightforward; the devil is in the details of the *tactics* of all the tiny steps that we can take to get from the awful bathos of the present War on Drugs to the agreeable conditions envisioned in several of the ten Parables. Herewith, dear reader, is my offering of ten Advocacies, practical little "pushes" that you can apply against the awesome (but perhaps, like Communism or Apartheid, ultimately brittle) edifice of the War:

Advocacy One: "We are all junkies"

Simple enough: just adopt a common language for all of the Big Seven substances. Thus, "I'm off to Starbucks to pick up my morning hit of caffeine", and "My daughter's a sugar junkie but at least I've gotten her into Diet Cokes", and "I've got a wine habit of two glasses daily with dinner". The aim is to affirm that we all enjoy using psychoactive substances– yes, even the Mormons, who forbade alcohol and tobacco and caffeine but got into sugar *big time*– and therefore we should drop any pretence of a social distance between the users of legal substances and the users of illicit "drugs".

Advocacy Two: Praise the mild, disparage the strong

For all the psychoactive substances of our lives, but especially the Big Seven, we need to sharpen our awareness of the *strength* of the stuff. So: If you love marijuana, disdain sinsemilla– it's too easy to overdo it on just one joint or even one toke. As for tobacco, consider rolling your own cigarettes, or smoking a pipe rather than a Marlboro. You'll use less, simply because you have to do just a little work for each dose. Go back to the old way of coffee– a 6-oz. ceramic cup rather than a 24-oz. Starbucks "vente". And "drop a dime" on your caffeine dealer– drop a dime into the cup of coffee, and if you can't see it thorugh an inch of liquid, perhaps it's too strong. As for the opiates– that is, the substance that best helps us feel no pain– learn about the forms which through history have done so with gentle moderation: a sip of laudanum syrup, a teaspoon of terpin hydrate of codeine, a half-pill of Percoset.

Advocacy Three: Demand that "small" be cheap

Keep an eye on *quantity* as well as strength. This especially applies to sugar drinks and to coffee. It seems that the smallest available quantity of Coke or Starbucks coffee is the 16-ounce "medium" or "tall" We can get by with less liquid! Make a point of demanding "small" from your caffeine or sugar-drink dealer– or carry an eight-ounce cup so that you can split the quantity (and the cost) of their smallest size with a friend.

Advocacy Four: Buy the local mildstuff

Just as you keep an eye on strength and quantity, also be vigilant about *source*. The stuff that comes from far away carries with it transportation costs (fuel, labor, road use, etc.) and perhaps import taxes as well. The local stuff is likely to be fresher and less refined. Perhaps you can't get your coffee or tea from a local grower, but many of us can actually visit a nearby winery, brewery, or pot farm. As for sugar– make regular stops at the local farmers' market, to see how much you can be tempted by the fresh fruits, berries, and honeys to be found there.

Advocacy Five: Work toward a tax structure that discriminates in favor of the mildstuff

Keep in mind the way the English resolved their Gin Plague in the mid-18th Century: they simply taxed gin heavily, and beer lightly. We do the same thing here and now, taxing hard liquor heavily ($1.20 per gallon of pure alcohol) and wine and beer lightly ($.19 per gallon).

Advocacy Six: Don't forget to tax sugar, too

Once the public understands that sugar products, like alcohol products, are simultaneously both "food" and "psychoactive substance", it becomes eminently logical that sugar be taxed in the same manner as alcohol. The milder forms of alcohol (beer and wine of less than 14% alcohol content) are taxed at a lesser rate than the stronger forms. Likewise, sugar can be taxed differentially, perhaps with "added sugar" bearing most or all of the burden.

There is plenty of precedent for taxing sugar. Import taxes were levied upon the 17th and 18th century trade. Closer to home, in 2002 Mexico started levying a 20% tax on soft drinks made with HFCS, as a means of protecting their domestic cane sugar industry against the importation of cheap American corn syrup. "Thanks to the tax, they [the American corn syrup industry] are sitting at the negotiating table", declared the president of Mexico's sugar industry association in 2005. "Without the tax, they would not even answer the telephone".

Advocacy Seven: Let usage be a shared experience

The advice of E.M. Forster, "only connect!" is the key. Share with your friends and family your consciousness of strength, quantity, and source of psychoactive substances. Speak frankly of your desires, delights, and troublesome overuse, and inquire gently into theirs. In bringing your kids into the pleasures of alcohol, be like a Mediterranean family: socialize them as adolescents with a little watered-down wine to share at meals.

Advocacy Eight: Free as many drug prisoners as possible

Vote against prison bonds. Rail against "wasteful government spending of our hard-earned tax dollars to arrest 750,000 people last year just for marijuana!" If on a jury, vote to acquit in drug-law violation cases. Support initiatives such as California's Proposition 36, which in five years has diverted more than 125,000 people away from prison and into treatment. And when the prisoners get free of the system, help them to get back on their feet. Don't let them be treated as second-class citizens.

Advocacy Nine: Work to overcome "pluralistic ignorance"

The majority of the American public agrees with most of the commonsensical substance use notions set forth in this book. But often it's hard to realize that, because the drug warriors have so dominated public forums, making policymakers hesitant to vote for reform lest they be called "soft on crime!" There are all sorts of ways that a reform-minded majority can become aware of itself: public opinion polls, radio call-in shows, website blogs, letters to the editor. So, speak your mind in public as best you can!

Advocacy Ten: Demand accountability

Hundreds of billions of dollars have been spent on the War on Drugs, locking up millions of people, disproportionately people of color. What a vast amount of *cruelty* and *waste* has been wrought upon our country! It's time to name names and hold policymakers responsible for action (or inaction) in allowing this cruelty and waste to persist. So– join the Drug Policy Alliance (www.drugpolicy.org) and add your voice to the rising cry for reform.

EPILOGUE

A Correspondence on Prohibition

December 7, 1996

Alan Leshner, Director
National Institute on Drug Abuse
Rockville, MD 20857

Dear Dr. Leshner,

At our breakfast meeting on Tuesday you quoted a sign in your office: "The definition of insanity is the repetition of unsuccessful behavior". Immediately I (and several others present) thought of the supreme example of unsuccessful behavior: the Nation's prohibition policies. We would love to know whether those policies are sometimes in your mind, too, when you look at your sign.

It would be a worthy project for NIDA to produce a consensus operational definition of "unsuccessful", so that we can objectively measure the success of our magnificent, costly drugs prohibition experiment. To find a clear negative outcome would enable the Nation, at last, seriously to consider the most obvious alternative behavior, recently summarized by *The Economist* in four words: "Legalize, regulate, tax, discourage". Of course, we might even then choose to persist in the unrewarded behavior, in which case we would be well served by historians to chronicle our collective "insanity".

Sincerely,

John Newmeyer, Ph.D.

******

December 20, 1996

Alan Leshner, Director
National Institute on Drug Abuse
Rockville, MD 20857

Dear Dr. Leshner,

Thank you for your thoughtful and articulate letter of December 16th.

You are correct that we dissenters have yet to prove our case. We have not fully documented the costs of prohibition, particularly

- the criminalization of huge numbers of Americans;
- the overburdening of courts and prisons;
- the reduction of quality of life and property values in our cities;
- the absence of potential revenues from sin taxes;
- the lack of regulatory limits on the potency, purity, and marketing of drugs; and
- the huge transfer of wealth to some rather nasty people.

Adequate documentation may take years, even decades, during which time documentation of the benefits of prohibition may also be pursued: worthy tasks to which to devote our professional lives, both at NIDA and out in the field. I'm reminded of Ho Chi Minh's comment that the ending of Western domination of Vietnam might require 100 years of struggle.

I remain interested in your private take on the War on Drugs: absolutely certain it must be continued, or open to consider alternatives?

Best wishes,

John Newmeyer

* * * * * *

January 1, 1997

Dear Alan,

Thanks very much for your letter of the 25th, relating the private views of yourself, Secretary Shalala, and Vice President Gore on the prohibition debate. I was surprised, but not astounded, by what I read.

Of course, you have my word of honor that I will keep the contents of your letter in the *strictest* confidence.

Warmly,

John

Closing Quotes

"I remember. I covered the Vietnam War. I remember the lies that were told, the lives that were lost– and the shock when, twenty years after the war ended, former Defense Secretary Robert S. McNamara admitted he knew it was a mistake all along. Today, our nation is fighting two wars, one abroad and one at home. While the war in Iraq is in the headlines, the other war is still being fought on our own streets. Its casualties are the wasted lives of our own citizens. I am speaking of the War on Drugs. And I cannot help but wonder how many more lives, and how much more money, will be wasted before another Robert McNamara admits what is plain for all to see: the War on Drugs is a failure."

Walter Cronkite
Open letter, February 20, 2006

"The War on Drugs has failed. And it's not just a failure of tactics, it's a failure of underlying strategy. Drug prohibition does little to combat the misuse of drugs. Instead it destroys communities, increases violent crime, tears apart families, and promotes the spread of infectious diseases. And as a result nearly half a million people are behind bars on drug charges. We simply cannot stand by and let this continue."

Ethan Nadelmann
Open letter, Drug Policy
Alliance, 2006

"In my work as a researcher on various projects we would obtain the analysis results and see distinct findings that had direct policy relevance. I had assumed, and was terribly disappointed to find otherwise, that policymakers and agency officials would attend to the results as an opportunity to improve policy and especially interventions. When this did not happen, and in my further experience where research was occasionally considered, I realized that the best a researcher could do was good, scientifically defensible work with the findings properly distributed both in presentations and publications. Thereafter, one had to be patient and be prepared as the sociopolitical context changed, as I have seen happen about every 15 or 20 years, to bring those research findings into the policy discussion."

M. Douglas Anglin
Interviewed by Richard
Rawson for *Addiction*, 2005